Everything I Understand
About America
I Learned in
Chinese Proverbs

Everything I Understand About America I Learned in Chinese Proverbs

Wendy Liu

HOMA & SEKEY BOOKS

PARAMUS, NEW JERSEY

FIRST EDITION

Library of Congress Cataloging-in-Publication Data

Liu, Wendy.
  Everything I understand about America I learned in Chinese proverbs / Wendy Liu. — 1st ed.
      p. cm.
  ISBN 978-1-931907-52-1 (pbk.)
  1. Liu, Wendy. 2. Chinese Americans—Biography. 3. National charac-teristics, American. 4. United States—Civilization. 5. United States—Relations—China. 6. China—Relations—United States. 7. Proverbs, Chinese. I. Title.
  E184.C5L654 2009
  305.895'1073—dc22
  [B]
                                    2008054385

Published by Homa & Sekey Books
3rd Floor, North Tower
Mack-Cali Center III
140 E. Ridgewood Ave.
Paramus, NJ 07652

Tel: 201-261-8810; 800-870-HOMA
Fax: 201-261-8890; 201-384-6055
Email: info@homabooks.com
Website: www.homabooks.com

Printed in the United States of America
1 3 5 7 9 10 8 6 4 2

Dedication

In memory of
my maternal grandmother
who never went to school but knew all the witty sayings.
She described my mother as someone
with a tongue as sharp as a knife but
a heart as soft as tofu.

TABLE OF CONTENTS

Part 4. US-China Relations

Preface

"You can take the girl out of the country, but not the country out of the girl," a friend once said to me, sarcastically, noticing something I did. Although I didn't think he was right specifically, he was in a broader sense. The country he was talking about was, of course, China.

I have lived in the United States for twenty years now. One thing I have found out is that my Chineseness has sometimes come out stronger away from China. It may be because of the contrast against all the Americanness around. Ease with things Chinese is only a small part of it. The bigger part, I would say, is Chinese thinking, especially with Chinese proverbs and sayings, perhaps the most intense form of Chineseness.

Jewels of Chinese language and crystals of Chinese wisdom, Chinese proverbs and sayings are rich, colorful, fun, philosophical, merciless sometimes, earthy at others, but always interesting. A love since girlhood, they helped shape my thinking in China yesterday and are influencing my understanding of America today. And I couldn't help it, when there were interesting stories, events, people and experiences begging to be summed up, that Chinese proverbs and sayings would pop up in my head.

Thus this collection of essays based on anecdotes and thoughts over the years in America filtered through some of my favorite Chinese proverbs and sayings.

Although they are Chinese, the morals in these proverbs and sayings are universal. And you don't have to take my word for it. With the popularity of China, Chinese proverbs and sayings have also become popular among Americans.

On his historic visit to China in 1972, President Nixon, for instance, started the trend by quoting a saying originated from one of Mao's poems: "一万年太久，只争朝夕。" (*yi wan nian tai jiu, zhi zheng zhao xi.*) or "Ten thousand years are too long. Seize the day, seize the moment."

Most Americans, of course, know this Chinese saying, "授人以鱼, 三餐之需。 授人以渔， 终生之用。" (*shou ren yi yu, san can zhi xu. shou ren yi yu, zhong sheng zhi yong.*) or "Give a man a fish, you feed him for a day. Teach a man to fish, you feed him for life."

But this book is not about Chinese proverbs and sayings. It is about the angle they provide to my understanding of America—its life, issues, politics, and China relations. Hope you find that angle interesting.

Hey, you might also find a favorite Chinese proverb or saying of your own!

Wendy Liu
Seattle, WA

Part 1. American Life

1. One Is Never Too Old to Be a Student

Chinese saying: 活到老, 学到老
Pronunciation: Huo Dao Lao, Xue Dao Lao
Translation: Living to Old Age and Learning to Old Age

I was already past the Big Three-O when I arrived in Atlanta from China to study for my master's degree. I felt old.

There was, first, the widely accepted Confucius' teaching in China that "One should be established by 30," meaning that one should have finished education and established one's career, family, outlook on life, etc. by that age, even though the ancient philosopher might have meant it only for men. Then there was the fact in China that colleges and universities rarely had students or graduate students over 30. Of course the Chinese always had the saying "Living to old age and learning to old age," but that "learning" was not exactly school learning, certainly not learning as a full-time student.

So it was quite a new thing to do to go back to school after 30. Yet there I was, starting an academic program at a ripe age, not to say in a different country. The youthful undergraduates all over the campus, on bikes, on skateboards, didn't help the case.

After the program started, however, I came to know several members of the program who were mid-career professionals, married, and even with kids. The most unusual was E, an energetic and friendly fellow. Not only was he taking more courses than anybody else in the program, he was also teaching part-time on campus and running a business on the side as well. What was most amazing about E was that he was about 60 years old and was the father-in-law of another member in the program! I was stunned, pleasantly. Hey, this

3

was the American style of "Living to old age and learning to old age," I told myself.

E impressed me further with his upbeat spirit through our conversations about the program, career, American society, etc., especially how he was having fun doing it all. There was not the slightest consideration of age.

Later on during the program, I came upon a television interview. The subject was a woman past 50. I do not remember her name, but I have never forgotten her words. She had just earned her law degree. The TV host asked why she had decided to go back to school and expected to earn a degree approaching 50. She said her family and friends had asked the same question. Her answer to them as well as the interviewer was the same: I am going to be 50 anyway no matter I get a degree or not. Why not with a degree?

Why not, indeed! What an extraordinary answer to age or learning at an older age?

I was truly moved by her story. I even felt a little ashamed of myself for feeling old as a student again after 30. But I definitely felt better and more confident about my studies afterwards.

Over the years, even long after I got my master's degree, I have been drawn to stories of "Living to old age and learning to old age" in America. Thousands of middle-aged men and women as well as senior citizens have gone back to school, to advance themselves, to change their careers, to pick up where they had left, to develop a new interest for their retirement years, etc.

The most inspiring story of older students had to be that of Mary Fasano. In 1997, at the age of 89, she became the oldest person to earn a bachelor's degree from Harvard.

Mary's education was interrupted when she was 14 years old. She had to work in a cotton mill to help her family, as the social as well as family tradition required of her. She promised herself, however, that one day she would go back to school. Years later when she was in her late 60s, with a successful diner business with her husband and their five children sent to college, she started working on her high school diploma. After earning it at age 71, she enrolled in Harvard and went on to work towards first an associate degree and then a bachelor's degree in liberal arts. 18 years of perseverance followed and paid off in the commencement season of 1997. Her whole family—5 children, 20 grandchildren and 18 great-grandchildren—joined to celebrate her achievement. "I am happy now," she said, "It is for my own satisfaction." I bet she was the happiest 89-year-old in the world that day!

Since then, two more ladies have broken Mary's record as well as the Guinness World Record: the 90-year-old Mozelle Richardson who received a Bachelor of Arts degree in Journalism from the University of Oklahoma in 2004; the 95-year-old Nola Ochs, earning a general studies degree with an emphasis on history from the Fort Hays Kansas State University in 2007.

In addition to these exceptional ladies who rendered us speechless, the trend-setting baby boomers have been turning "back to school" from a novelty to a fact of life. According to one AOL report, at the beginning of 2007, there were 80,000 baby boomers taking classes along with 18-year-olds. Experts say that, baby boomers, already the most educated generation, desire to remain connected to the workforce and make intellectual contributions as they near retirement age, or for pure enjoyment. One 56-year-old successful business executive has been pursuing another degree: MBA. Why? She said she wanted to make herself a more valuable asset to her firm and her family.

In her and all those older students, I have seen not only shining examples of the Chinese saying "Living to old age and learning to old age" but also that of the English saying "One is as old as one feels."

With these examples, it seems odd that I even felt old being a graduate student after 30. With these examples, I doubt that anyone of us can ever have anything to say about being too old to learn or too old to be a student again.

ॐ　　ॐ　　ॐ　　ॐ　　ॐ

2. Looking for the Three Major Differences in America

Chinese saying: 消灭三大差别
Pronunciation: Xiao Mie San Da Cha Bie
Translation: Eliminate the Three Major Differences

Not strictly a traditional Chinese saying, "Eliminate the three major differences" could be called a socialist Chinese saying. It was so much part of the political jargon in the pre-reform China of the 1960-70s that it became a special saying for my generation.

The three major differences were those between urban and rural areas, between industry and agriculture, and between mental and manual work. One goal of socialism, as we learned, was to develop a society without those three major differences. Ideally it would be a communist society.

Anyone who grew up in China in the 1960s and 70s knew how different the Chinese countryside was from the cities: no running water, no paved roads, no toilet, and in many cases, no electricity.

Early in the summer, we city folks would go to the countryside to help with the wheat harvest. For a week or two, we worked and lived alongside our peasant hosts: bundling harvested wheat, loading them onto handcarts, pulling or pushing them out of the fields, drinking water from a big bowl, eating steamed corn bread, going to the bathroom in a pigsty, sleeping on a brick bed, etc.

Fast-forward to the late 1980s, in Atlanta, when I got to see the American countryside.

The "countryside" was in West Georgia. It was a farm owned by a friend and his family. The friend was a well-known judge. And "Judge" was not only the position he had held for many years, it was also how the locals called him.

At the time I was in Atlanta, Judge had already retired from the court. But he was still working at the law firm that he owned together with his two lawyer sons. The office building was in the county seat, about 20 minutes' drive from his home on the farm. The sons were married and had their own homes elsewhere. But Judge had always lived on the farm. Besides responsibilities at the law firm, Judge and his wife took care of the farm.

The farm was very large, with plots of corn, vegetables, and cherry trees, along with several lakes, one pond of catfish, plus acres of timber and pecan trees. It was not just a farm. There was also a ranch, with several hundred heads of cattle and goats pasturing on the rising and falling green. That was not all. There were also chickens and pigs. The most interesting animals on the farm, however, were peacocks, and peahens, of course. Honestly, it was the first time I ever saw peacocks walking freely and leisurely outside a zoo!

For all the work on the farm, from planting to harvesting, from buying to selling, from construction work to machinery work, Judge had but one manager. Early in the morning, Judge would drive around inspecting the farm before going to the law office. In the evening, Judge would change into his work overalls, look around again and talk to the manager, learning about the day's development and making decisions about the next day's work and hire, etc. While he was away during the day, "Mrs. Judge" supervised the manager and contractors.

The house Judge and his wife lived in had been built by Judge's father. It was a white, two-storied building, with a grand magnolia tree in the front, reminding one of the scenes in the movie *Gone with the Wind*. Everything inside was modern, of course, as any house in Atlanta.

There was a church down the road, also built by Judge's father. On Sunday mornings, Judge would rise early to go to the church, first thing, to start the electric bell there. The ring, like music, would ripple far and wide through the misty air.

The picture, not just of the church, challenged my Chinese mind beyond limit: A retired judge running both a law firm and a farm on a daily basis, going to cattle meetings, planning an irrigation system, meeting friends at a country club, attending fund raisers, looking after a family church on weekends, in a word, changing from suit and tie into yellow overalls so naturally and seamless... Where were the three major differences?

To me, Judge was one man of all three pairs of opposites, or one man who resolved the three opposites: urban vs. rural, industrial vs. agricultural, and mental vs. manual.

If the elimination of the three major differences was a mark of a communist society, America the capitalist seemed to have come closer to it than China the socialist. If the elimination of the three major differences meant combining rural and urban, agricultural and industrial, manual and mental, Judge was its poster boy.

The image of a peacock taking a walk is still vivid in my head when I think back to Judge and West Georgia.

✍ ✍ ✍ ✍ ✍

9

3. Freedom to Be Homeless in America?

Chinese proverb: 无家可归
Pronunciation: Wu Jia Ke Gui
Translation: Wandering about with No Home to Go To

Americans are proud of many things, from their freedom to their opportunities. But there is one thing Americans can't say they are proud of—the homeless, or those "wandering about with no home to go to" as the Chinese proverb describes.

When I was in Atlanta in the late 1980s, the city was experiencing a continuous economic growth. Job opportunities attracted people from all over the United States. At the same time, the homeless population grew, too. It was as high as 10,000 at one time.

As an international student on a bus tour around the town one day, it was quite a sobering experience for me to see a line of people standing in the street and to learn that it was the soup kitchen line for the homeless.

It was even more shocking later to hear that when the two-term Mayor Andrew Young went out on the street in downtown Atlanta, dressed "up" as a homeless person and begged, no one even recognized him!

Again, working in Washington D.C as an intern one summer, I saw homeless people around the National Mall and near the Library of Congress. It was hard to believe. Homeless in the capital of the richest nation on earth!?

To many Democrats, the serious homeless problem was the result of large cuts in welfare programs under the Reagan years. To many Republicans, it was the homeless themselves who rather lived on welfare, or on street, than taking minimum wage jobs.

After I moved to Seattle, I noticed the homeless again. Even though voted "the Best Place to Live" by Money magazine in 1990, the city was no better place to live for the homeless. Of a total of 5,000 homeless persons that year, 100 of them put up tents outside the city stadium one day to draw attention and protest. They did get the attention of the then Mayor Norm Rice. With the help of the mayor as well as charity organizations, they were able to move into some "new housing." But the arrangement was only temporary and benefited only a small number of the homeless in Seattle. While in Washington state as a whole, during the fiscal year of 1990, 50,000 people had reportedly used the 120 homeless shelters!

According to statistics released by U.S. Conference of Mayors that year, of the national homeless population, 52% were single men, 34% were families with children, 12% were single women, 46% were blacks, 34% white, 15% Hispanics, 3% American Indian and 1% Asian.

Why were they homeless? One analysis pointed out that the homeless fate often came suddenly with an unfortunate turn in one's life. It could be the loss of one's job, a disease, fire, divorce, etc. Without savings, insurance, or family and friends to turn to, one could soon get the taste of a homeless life. According to another study by the Conference for 2000, the causes of homelessness included the lack of affordable housing, substance abuse, mental illness, domestic violence, poverty, low paying jobs and changes in public assistance.

The saddest fact about the homeless was that many of them were veterans, including the Vietnam War veterans, who had risked their lives, shed blood, lost limbs or a sound mind for this country. One survey by the Urban Institute in the late 1990s found that veterans accounted for 23% of all homeless people in America.

11

Not only was their make-up telling, the size of the homeless population was also grave. In 1996, it was estimated between 640,000 to 840,000 by the Urban Institute. In its 2000 report, the Institute said that at least 2.3 million adults and children, or nearly 1 percent of the U.S. population, were likely to experience a spell of homelessness at least once during year. In 2005, according to the Department of Housing and Urban Development, there were 754,147 people that were homeless, living in shelters, transitional housing, and on streets.

Those were shocking statistics, shocking because they posed a shocking question: How could homelessness, or people "wandering about with no home to go to," and America, the richest nation, two completely opposite and logically unrelated phenomena, co-exist for so long?

I am not sure who is right or better in finding a solution to the problem: The Democrats who prefer more public programs, or the Republicans who prefer more personal responsibilities. As a well-known Chinese proverb suggests, giving a man a fish feeds him for a day, teaching a man to fish feeds him for life. Maybe the solution should be a combination of the two?

It is, however, easier said than done, while the homeless problem persists. As I was finalizing this manuscript, a new homeless camp with 150 tents made front page in Seattle. Was it déjà vu of twenty years ago, or a reflection of the new financial reality? Just reading about it made me feel at a loss, not to say when I recalled the words of a friend back in Atlanta: "America is a free country. You have the freedom to be homeless."

      * * * * *

4. You Are "Master" in Public Libraries

Chinese proverb: 当家作主
Pronunciation: Dang Jia Zuo Zhu
Translation: Being Master in One's Own House

China's economy used to be almost 100% public owned. Everything was government run, from factories to schools, from theaters to department stores, from trains to buses, and from parks to libraries. The Chinese citizens were, of course, "masters in their own house" of socialist China.

But when you lived in a public-ownership society, you rarely stopped to think of the meaning behind "public," or how much of a "master" you were. Take libraries for example, public libraries, of course.

It was in the pre-reform days. There was a provincial library in Xi'an, the capital of Shaanxi province and my hometown. It was a public library no doubt, but not for everyone of the "public." To obtain a library card there, one had to have a certain level of education or employment, a letter of official introduction from one's work unit, a formal application, which then needed to be approved by the library. The process would take days or weeks. Once you had the card, there was a limit to the number of items you could check out. The higher the rank of your education or employment, the more items you could check out.

With a college degree and a staff job at a governmental agency, I was lucky to have been qualified, and obtained a card from this particular library. My limit was two items in science and technology category, and one in literature category. For the former, I could keep the items for a month. For the latter, it was half a month.

I had lived in two more cities in China and had similar experience with the libraries. In the last one, Shenzhen, however, I finally saw change coming in the late 1980s. The Shenzhen Public Library announced that it would issue a library card to anyone who wished to have it. I didn't know the details. But I saw a mob in front of the library one day and learned that it was the first day of the new issuance.

With that experience and memory, I came upon the Seattle Public Library booth one day a few years later. It was on a Fourth of July in a park by the Elliott Bay. There were concerts, games, food, craft, as well as booths of various organizations or services. In front of the Seattle Public Library booth was a desk and a sign that said, "Get your Seattle Public Library card here." It was very inviting.

I walked up, a little hesitantly, and asked the lady by the desk who could get a card. Immediately after asking the question, I felt stupid, really stupid. She smiled and said, anyone who lived in the Seattle area. Do you live in Seattle? She asked. Yes, I answered. She gave me a simple form to fill, name and address, etc., and told me to check my mail in the next few days.

I did. A red plastic Seattle Public Library card, my first American public library card, arrived a few days later, just as the lady said! I could check out as many items, or categories, as I wanted. I could call to place hold on any item I needed and it would be mailed to me when available. I could also check out items at any branch of the library and return them at another branch. It was all so easy and convenient. Wow!

Later on, of course, I learned to use other public libraries, and online, and have been enjoying them all these years.

It was indeed stupid but true that it was only when I got the Seattle Public Library card did I begin to appreciate the meaning of "public" in America: By living here, consuming here, and paying taxes here, you were the public. In fact, you were part owner of the public libraries, as well as other public institutions or facilities built and maintained with taxpayers' money, and therefore entitled to their free services. In a word, as the Chinese proverb "being master in your own house" suggests, you were truly master in your own public library house.

Still, it was interesting how in the once all "public" China, public institutions were not really all public. While in the mostly private America, public institutions were truly public.

Now, of course, the ever-larger economy in China means ever-bigger expenditure on public institutions such as libraries. I don't think any young person in China today knows what it was like to obtain a library card in my days. They would certainly not embarrass themselves by asking the silly question as to who could get a card from an American public library.

⟡   ⟡   ⟡   ⟡   ⟡

5. Negative Role Models and Our Children

Chinese proverb: 上梁不正下梁歪
Pronunciation: Shang Liang Bu Zheng Xia Liang Wai
Translation: If the Upper Beam Is Not Straight,
the Lower Ones Will Go Askew

After the Clinton-Lewinsky affair broke out in 1998, there was a lot of debate over whether a president was a role model. Many Americans believed that a president was not a role model. They said that as long as a president was doing a good job, his private life, even immoral, was not our business. They suggested, therefore, people, especially young people, should look for role models in their own homes, schools, churches and communities, not in the Oval Office. I both agreed and disagreed with this view.

The Chinese proverb in the title concerning beams may sound like a piece of advice for housing construction. It is in fact one for proper behavior. What it really says is that when members of the upper beams of a society or organization behave unworthily, those of the lower ones would behave unworthily as well. The upper-beam members, I would say, could include political leaders, business leaders, community leaders, celebrities, etc. The lower-beam ones could be the average men and women, old and young. When it comes to a community and a household, adults would certainly be the upper beams and children the lower ones.

Children are like sponges. They absorb, imitate and copy adults' behavior, positive or negative, real or fictional. We could probably all remember, also in 1998, the school shooting that involved two young boys, one 11 and another 13, in Jonesboro, Arkansas. Where did the boys learn to kill innocent people with guns? From the grown-ups, of course. With frequent news stories of some lone gunman walking into a school, a restaurant, or an office, and starting to shoot, and with television shows and movies depicting and glorifying gun violence, it was obvious where kids had picked up the idea. In their tender minds, images of those gunmen and the momentary gratification from killing could be heroic.

It was technically correct to say that President Clinton was not a role model, and by extension, those adult gunmen were not role models, either. But the problem was that even if a president or those adult gunmen were not declared role models, by holding the highest office of the land or just being grown-ups in the society, they were de facto role models, and their behavior had effect on the public. Unfortunately, President Clinton, with his affair, and those gunmen, with their crimes, had served as negative role models, especially for our young people.

The same argument continued then onto other members of the upper beams of the society—sports stars, for instance. They were not role models, people said. They themselves never said they were, either. One basketball star even came out and made an announcement on television that he was not a role model and that kids should not look up to him, etc.

That was easily said. It may also be true. Just as politicians didn't win a public office to be our role models, neither did NBA players reach the peak of their game to become role models for our kids. But when a politician or a basketball player, a business leader or an actor, achieved high power, authority and fame, enjoyed wide visibility, publicity and celebrity, and became an icon, he or she automatically, willingly or not, took on an implied responsibility to be a good person, a straight upper beam of the society, and a role model. When they engaged in immoral behavior, the negative influence was on the whole society, especially the young. When the resident of the White House did that, the negative effect was on all houses in America, blue, brown, gray or green.

That's why it bothered me a little back then when I learned that many Americans, especially baby-boomers like President Clinton himself, with young kids at home, didn't think too much of the White House scandal. Did they consider the kind of message they were sending to our kids or the kind of upper beams we had in place in the house of the nation?

A tilted upper beam makes the lower ones to go askew. The beams askew in below reflect the tilted beam above. Together they tell the structural problem of a house. Therefore, on the one hand, those adult gunmen served as negative role models for the young school gunmen. On the other, the tolerance of the negative example of President Clinton with his inglorious behavior reflected the moral picture of the American society.

A strong house would need all its beams straight, upper or lower. But upper-beam members, starting from the president of the United States, undoubtedly shoulder a larger responsibility, responsibility to be positive role models. They have to be straight first and set a good example for the lower-beam members, the young people in particular, so America's moral house would stay straight and strong, not tilt or collapse.

    ✿   ✿   ✿   ✿   ✿

6. It Takes Years for a Boy to Grow into a School Shooter

Chinese proverb: 冰冻三尺, 非一日之寒
Pronunciation: Bing Dong San Chi Fei Yi Ri Zhi Han
Translation: It Takes More Than One Cold Day
for a River to Freeze Three Feet Deep

It is perhaps one of the most tragic and terrifying terms in modern English vocabulary as well as a news item: school shooting. It is tragic and terrifying for those who had to find out that their children were injured or killed in a school shooting. It is more tragic and terrifying for those who had to find out that their child was the gunman in a school shooting.

I first wrote an opinion on school shooting in my local paper back in the late 1990s, a peak period of school shootings. There was the Frontier Junior High shooting in Moses Lake, Washington in 1996; the Heath High School shooting, West Paducah, Kentucky in 1997; the Westside Middle School shooting in Jonesboro, Arkansas; the Thurston High School shooting in Springfield, Oregon in 1998; and of course, the Columbine High School massacre in Littleton, Colorado in 1999. The shootings did not stop in subsequent years. They just did not take on the scale of the Virginia Tech massacre in April 2007, which, with its record number of victims, highlighted once more, as more than ever, the tragedy and terror of school shootings.

We all know how, after each incident of a school shooting, representatives from the media, schools, government, community, etc. would go on television and newspapers trying to explain what went wrong. At the same time, as David Brooks of the *New York Times* wrote after the Virginia Tech shooting, neuroscientists, evolutionary psychologists and social scientists would explain from fields of biology, chemistry and social science the behavior of the school shooters. Brooks himself, however, wanted to know where background forces should stop and individual choice and responsibility should begin in analyzing what went wrong with these young gunmen.

What indeed went wrong? There seemed to be a lot that did, as suggested by specialists and pundits over the years.

Guns? Some pointed out that it was the easy availability of guns, without adequate background checks. It was certainly true in the Virginia Tech case in which Seung-Hui Cho easily purchased two semi-automatic guns, even though he had had a history of mental illness.

Violent culture? Some pointed out that it was the violent culture that permeated American youngsters' everyday life. Violent movies and video/computer games glorifying characters armed with automatic and futuristic weapons and blood-spilling powers gave them a false impression that killing was heroic, macho and fun.

Sociopath? Some pointed out these young gunmen were simply sociopathic, bizarre, sick, and abnormal, maybe because they had been abused, disturbed, unloved, and just lonely.

School neglect? Some pointed out that it was the schools that had neglected the signs. These young gunmen were all said to have either given verbal or written threats or showed signs of potential danger before the shooting. The signs were, however, ignored or not taken seriously.

Media? Some pointed out that it was the media that had always sensationalized such shooting rampages and turned them into something impressionable and troubled youngsters wanted to copycat.

Although no one single reason offered could explain America's school shootings, together they provided various parts to the problem. However, there was one very important part that was missing from these arguments, one that I believed could be the underlying factor in all these young criminal activities, namely: parenting, or lack of it.

The Chinese proverb in the title says, "It takes more than one cold day for a river to freeze three feet deep." What it suggests is that bad things do not just happen accidentally one day. The trouble usually has brewed for quite some time before its breakout. America's schoolyard gunmen were certainly not born that way. It took years for them to grow into school shooters and mass murderers. It took 11 years and 13 years, respectively, for Andrew Golden and Mitchell Johnson of Jonesboro; 14 years for Barry Loukaitis of Moses Lake; 15 years for Kip Kinkel of Springfield; 17 and 18 years respectively for Dylan Bennet Klebold and Eric David Harris of Columbine; and 23 years for Virginia Tech's Seung-Hui Cho. As most of them were teenagers, an obvious question rose: Where were their parents?

Who brought the children into this world? The parents. Whom do our children spend most time with from their first cry at the birth center to the day they leave for college? The parents. Children are, of course, the wealth and future of the society. But before they reach adulthood, they are their parents' children. They are named Johnson, Loukaitis, Klebold, and Harris, not Frontier Junior High or Columbine High. Therefore, parents bear more responsibility, also more years of responsibility, in raising their children into good and law-abiding citizens.

To reach that goal, raising children should be much more than feeding them, clothing them, sheltering them, sending them to school, driving them to after-school activities, giving them spending money, taking them on vacations, and even asking "How's school today?" at the dinner table, if there is a dinner at the table.

21

All parents love their children naturally. But that is not enough. There are three aspects I could think of as very important in parenting.

One. Parents should make an effort to be their children's friends, best friends if possible, friends who can trust each other and talk about things. Otherwise, why would children want to confide in their parents or discuss with their parents anything that is really going on in their minds or lives?

Two. Parents should try their best to be their children's role models in everyday life, from work to love, from responsibility to morality, from obeying laws to respecting other people, from community service to political activism, from care about the environment to care about the world, etc.

Three. Parents should also, and have to, be good observers of their children, and pay close attention to children's behavioral changes, from day to day, week to week. That way, the parents would be able to nip in the bud anything in their children that might go wrong.

It was a little late for those parents to find it hard to talk to their child about anything, or find it necessary to get counseling or medication for their child's strange mood. It was late when they got a call from the police department that their child was being questioned or charged. It was certainly too late when they saw their child on television identified as the gunman in a school shooting.

Brooks was right to emphasize individual responsibility in these young gunmen. But as another Chinese proverb about long-term effect says, "It takes ten years to grow trees, but a hundred to rear people." It was the parents who should have cultivated in their children a sense of individual responsibility in the first place and made sure the children maintain that sense throughout their growing years.

It was tragedy that Seung-Hui Cho's parents felt that they didn't know their son who committed the Virginia Tech massacre. But their son was with them all his younger years. After all, as a river didn't freeze three feet deep in one day, a boy didn't grow into a school shooter in one day, either.

          ✿   ✿   ✿   ✿   ✿

7. America's TV and Radio—Showcase of Free Speech

**Chinese proverb: 知无不言, 言无不尽, 言者无罪, 闻者足戒
Pronunciation: Zhi Wu Bu Yan, Yan Wu Bu Jin,
Yan Zhe Wu Zui, Wen Zhe Zu Jie
Translation: Say All You Know, Say It Without Reserve,
Blame Not the Speaker, but Be Warned by His Words**

When you see the Chinese proverb above, "Say all you know, say it without reserve, blame not the speaker, but be warned by his words," you would think that it is a pretty good recipe for free speech and an open society. But you probably would never have guessed that it had been used as a tactic in a series of political movements in China, especially under Mao Zedong, the late leader of the Chinese Communist Party, to rout out rivals or dissidents.

By "saying all you know and saying it without reserve" during an inner party rectification movement in the 1940s, a large number of party members, including high-ranking members, got purged. By "saying all you know and saying it without reserve" during the Anti-Rightist movement in the 1950s, hundreds of thousands of people, party members and non-party members, were labeled Rightists and banished to labor camps. Then there was the decade-long political nightmare in the 1960s-70s called the Great Proletarian Cultural Revolution, in which everybody had to follow Mao quotations and party speech, ultimately making speaking one's mind the most costly and foolish thing to do in China.

Although those large-scale, ultra-left, political movements are a memory now, the age-old Chinese proverb about free speech is yet to be fully realized.

The great irony is that this age-old Chinese proverb is a

reality in the United States. Freedom of speech, the most valued of rights in America, is guaranteed in the First Amendment of the U.S. Constitution and practiced every day cross
the land. It is also the most attractive benefit of being or becoming an American, especially for an immigrant from a socialist and/or totalitarian country.

I could never forget this joke from the Cold War years:
an American visitor told a Soviet citizen that he, the American, could stand in a public square in Washington, DC, for
instance, and shout "Down with President So and So!" The
Soviet citizen replied that he could do that, too, in Moscow.
The difference was, of course, that he, the Soviet, could shout
"Down with" the American president, but not his own. The
same conversation could have taken place in Beijing.

Americans, of course, have always been able to criticize
or ridicule their president or any public figure anytime anywhere in any way. The level of the freedom to speak in America has amazed me. From politicians to private citizens, from
newspaper columnists to magazine publishers, no one had to
pull his or her punches in expressing their views. For me, a
news junkie, the most impressive examples of that freedom
have been the TV and radio news talk shows, the most visible
and audible form of free speech.

Over the years, I have followed a number of news talk
shows including *This Week with Sam and Cokie* on ABC (later
This Week with George Stephanopoulos), *The McLaughlin Group* on
PBS, *Crossfire* on CNN, *Meet the Press* on NBC, *The O'Reiley
Factor* on FOX, *The Rush Limbaugh Show* on the radio, and the
somewhat different *The Daily Show with Jon Stewart* on Comedy
Central.

The most interesting one, and my favorite, has to be *The
McLaughlin Group*. This fast paced, highly contentious, quick
thinking and tightly structured show is also a shouting match.
The four panelists, two from the right and two from the left,
almost always talk at the same time, each trying to shout

down the other or he or she would lose the opportunity to speak. Mr. McLaughlin, the moderator with a great sense of humor, always asks the panelists to rate an event, its impact or its probability, from 0 to 10 or by A, B, C, and D. He then settles the issue with his own arbitrary final answer. It is great fun watching it.

The most outrageous is perhaps *The Rush Limbaugh Show* on the radio. Limbaugh is so conceited that he calls his program the Limbaugh Institute of Advanced Conservative Studies and his network EIB, or Excellence In Broadcasting. Even though I listened to him only for a period of time, I was really impressed by his knowledge of American politics, especially conservative politics. He was also such a good talker that I wouldn't hesitate to give him this very fitting Chinese description: One with a three-inch tongue that never wears out.

The most heated of all news talk shows was probably *Crossfire* on CNN. It was a great pity that it had to go off the air. With two hosts representing the two mainstream political camps plus one or more guests seated in the middle, the show pitched the right against the left and vice versa, with quick-fire arguments from the two sides clashing and sparking in close range, like a verbal hand-to-hand combat. It was truly a great form of political debate. I hope the show would not only return to the air someday, but also be extended to one hour instead of 30 minutes.

The most hilarious is no doubt *The Daily Show with Jon Stewart*. Combining news and issues with pungent and merciless satire, Stewart makes fun of everybody in the news, Republican or Democrat, American or foreign, president or God. With all the heavy news in the world today, he provides viewers half an hour to lighten up and laugh a little. Through tons of news stories every day, he cuts to the heart of an issue and exposes its stupidity or absurdity. It is a rare ability of Stewart's to see, and show, the funny side of a most serious event.

I like these news talk shows first for their intellectual level, their range and depth of coverage, their style and structure of presentation, and their colorful hosts and guests. I like them more for what they stand for: a highly concentrated form of free speech, offering the public lively, heated, face-to-face and tit-for-tat discussions or debates over the more important matters in America. Talk radio is even more direct and accessible than television ones. It gives listeners and callers up-to-minute analysis of and an on-going forum on local as well as national news and issues.

The most important reason I have enjoyed these news talk shows, on television or radio, is what they reminded me of: "Say all you know, say it without reserve, blame not the speaker, but be warned by his words," the Chinese proverb about free speech. On these shows, every one, host, panelist, guest, or caller, can speak without reserve, on political issues of the day or political leaders of the moment, and no one gets blamed for what he or she says. They are a true realization, in America, not in its homeland, of the old proverb. They have also made me wonder if China would ever have their own wise McLaughlin, conceited Rush Limbaugh, and funny Stewart.

There has been, of course, sea change in today's China in terms of personal freedom, including freedom of speech. However, it is one thing to be able to "say all you know and say it without reserve" about jobs, schools, traffic, sports, marriage, sex, corruption, environment, even local politics and foreign affairs, it is quite another to be able to "say all you know, say it without reserve" about national politics, national leaders, especially political reform.

Free speech won't be really free in China until Chinese citizens can say all they know and say it without reserve about all politics, and can shout "Down with" their own president, if they want to, in Tiananmen Square. Free speech won't be truly free in China until the second part of the age-old proverb is also a reality: where not only can one say all one knows, say it without reserve, but also say it without being blamed, harassed, detained or even jailed.

8. Blame It All on Satan

Chinese saying: 走火入魔
Pronunciation: Zou Huo Ru Mo
Translation: Going Too Far and Becoming Delusional

To many Americans, atheist may sound alien or bad. But I am one, as most people from China are. Evolution and historical/dialectical materialism were part of my education. I learned and agreed with the lyrics of Internationale, the anthem of international socialism, "There has never been any savior of the world,/ Nor God, nor Emperors on which to depend./ To create Mankind's happiness,/ We must entirely depend on ourselves!" I was also familiar with Karl Marx' famous words on religion: the opium of the masses; the illusory happiness of the people.

An education in China no doubt played a part in my outlook. But after two decades of living in the United States, with the freedom to join or believe in any religion, I remain an atheist. There may have been a number of reasons. The overwhelming one is, believe it or not, "Been there, done that."

Even though the Chinese were mostly unreligious, they treated their "supreme" leader Mao Zedong like a god. Even though I was never a religious person, I lived through political fanaticism like one. In America, organized worshipping of God reminded me of organized worshiping of Mao. Following the Bible to the letter reminded me of following Mao's Little Red Book to the character. Expressions of love for God reminded me of expressions of love for Mao. Unconditional faith in God reminded me of unconditional faith in Mao. God and Mao may be different, but the devotion to them seemed much the same.

29

One similarity struck me more than others: Christians would credit God for all that was good in the world, just as the Chinese had once credited Mao for all that was good in China; Christians would blame Satan for anything that was bad, just as the Chinese had once blamed Mao's enemies for anything that was bad in China. However, it was the way Christians explained death, which Mao's followers had never attempted, that made me feel incredulous. It reminded me of this Chinese saying: "*Zou huo ru mo*," or "Going too far and becoming delusional."

"Going too far and becoming delusional" as an expression is originated from *qi gong*, or exercise of deep breathing. When *qi gong* is done excessively or incorrectly, a person would be unable to come out of the state of exercise. Instead, he or she could be trapped in a state of confusion in his or her thoughts, emotion and behavior. That's the condition called "Going too far and becoming delusional." The saying is used to describe someone who is going too far, becoming delusional and getting lost in something: an exercise, a belief, or a superstition.

In November 1998, John Stanford, the Seattle Public School Superintendent, a can-do hero all his life, well respected and loved, died of leukemia. All the therapies and surgeries and prayers couldn't save him. He was gone, to the grief of the Seattle public.

Moved by the story, I asked a question, from the point of view of most Americans but also challenging it: Why would an all-loving, all-caring, omnipotent and omniscient supernatural entity allow this to happen?

I did not, of course, ask the question at home, I did it in my opinion column in the local paper, seeking wisdom from readers. I got a free lesson on Satan.

It came in a long email from a Christian reader. It pointed out why I should not have even begun to contemplate such a question. It said that terrible diseases were not the doings of God. They were the doings of Satan, the chief of evil spirit, the enemy of God and the great adversary of man. Satan was always out there trying to get people to turn against God and disobey him. The email then assured me that God was much more powerful and far greater than Satan, or any other demon, and that God could always protect us. So, did God protect the superintendent? Or did Satan beat God in this case?

I also received a book of questions about God for children. I guessed it was good for children of all ages. So I turned to the question, "Why does God let us get sick?" and found this answer: "Sometimes sickness is the body's way of telling us that we should stop living a certain way... Sickness and diseases are problems that came into the world with sin... And when we are sick, we can pray to God and ask him to help us." So, did the superintendent live a certain way associated with sin? Did God answer Seattle's prayer for the superintendent?

In the summer of 1999, John Kennedy, Jr. died in a plane crash. The news shocked and grieved Americans. All kinds of people were interviewed on television to shed light on the tragedy. The Rev. Billy Graham was on ABC's Good Morning America one day. He was asked this question by the anchor, "What would you say to the Kennedy family to comfort them if you were with them?" Billy Graham replied, "I would tell them that God loved them. God has a plan for everything. This was all planned. Everything happens for a purpose." Really?

Thirty-six years earlier, in 1963, President Kennedy was assassinated, with his youthful and promising presidency cut short. The scene of that fatal moment, shown so many times on television, was deeply etched on America's collective mind.

In 1968, civil rights leader Martin Luther King was also assassinated. I had read his famous speech "I Have A

Dream" as a student in China. Imagine how much more an eloquent and natural leader like King could have accomplished had he lived on.

Then there was Princess Diana, in 1997. Championing a number of noble causes in the world, Diana earned the nickname Queen of Hearts. Yet, she had to die in a car accident, having failed to find the love that had eluded her in marriage, and leaving two young sons behind.

Now John Kennedy, Jr. Though not into politics yet, he had started a popular political magazine, trying to live up to his famous family name and his mother's expectations. Yet, he had to die so young in a plane crash, ending his dreams as well as fellow Americans' for him.

Were all these tragedies part of God's plan as Rev. Billy Graham told Good Morning America? I raised the point again in my column.

Of course not, my answer came. "God did not plan for them to die. That was Satan's plan," one woman wrote in a letter to the editor. She stated that she was expressing her views and those who shared the same views. She pointed out that I shouldn't have asked God why. The one I should have been asking was Satan. She went on to explain that God would not take good people who made life worthwhile on this planet before their time, or anyone before their journey through life on this planet Earth was through. For those who chose not to listen to God, she comforted, it was never too late to turn it around and become one of the good people. As for my doubt if we still had any control of our life if everything was planned by God, the letter said, "The answer is yes when we choose not to listen to Satan."

I guess, according to her, those who hadn't been able to control their lives, or the sudden end of their lives, must have listened to Satan. That would have included JFK, Martin Luther King, Princess Diana, John Kennedy, Jr., John Stanford,

32

and thousands upon thousands of people either inflicted with incurable diseases or killed in fatal accidents.

Well, as an atheist, I would opt for the more worldly and practical causes of these tragedies. President Kennedy and Martin Luther King, Jr. died from assassins' bullets. There were obvious political as well as security issues involved. Princess Diana and John Kennedy, Jr. died of accidents. More caution and better judgment might have made a difference. As for those unfortunate diseases, hereditary or acquired, new and better medicine would surely bring cure or alleviation in the future.

I am not sure how Marx came to make his famous opium comment. But religion, Christianity in this case, did seem to have a tranquilizing effect on its believers, making them see and accept things, especially life and death, in simplified terms of God and Satan. To me, that was a little "Going too far and becoming delusional." But again, I kind of knew what it was like. There was once a lot of "Going too far and becoming delusional" in China, with Mao.

9. The Internet and Instant Scholars

Chinese saying: 秀才不出门，全知天下事
Pronunciation: Xiu Cai Bu Chu Men, Quan Zhi Tian Xia Shi
Translation: A Scholar Knows the World Without Stepping Out His Door

A *xiu cai* was an ancient Chinese scholar who had passed the imperial exams and was qualified to become a civil servant. *Xiu cais* were a greatly respected and admired group. They were the ones who had read and even memorized everything in the Four Books and Five Classics, etc. and knew all the affairs under the Heaven. They were also the ones who brought glory to their village or clan. People were amazed that *xiu cais* could know everything about the world just by reading books. Thus the proverb.

In modern China, the term *xiu cai* has become a general term for a scholar, a good student, or a good writer. There was an unfortunate twist of fate, however, for the term during the tumultuous years of the Cultural Revolution. Mao believed that China's education had become bourgeois and needed to be smashed and rebuilt. Schools were closed. Books considered not in line with Marxist and Maoist teachings were either banned or destroyed. Scholars and good students of the "old" system were labeled "black *xiu cais*," as opposed to "red" and "revolutionary" ones. It was assumed that the more book knowledge one had, the more counterrevolutionary one would become. Fortunately, that revolution is long over. *Xiu cai* is again a complimentary rather than a derogatory term for a learned person.

But no matter how much of the world's affairs ancient *xiu cais* could know, they could never have dreamed of the instant availability of all kinds of information, knowledge as well as learning tools such as dictionaries, encyclopedia, etc. on the Internet in the late 20th century. They could never have imagined that everyone could now know all about world affairs without stepping out of their door, or away from their computer.

I still remember the amazement I felt using a campus e-mail account in gradate school in Atlanta in the late 1980s to communicate with my professors and fellow students and search the school library. But that was no comparison to the Internet. When I became a member of AOL in the early 1990s, I was blown away.

I was blown away not only because of the Chinese proverb the Internet reminded me of as it turned everyone into an instant *xiu cai*, or scholar, with ready access to so much of the world at one's finger tip, it blew me away with its magic and power.

The Internet is magic because it performs all tasks, like a mother of all jacks-of-all-trades. It is an omnipotent tool for everything we do: from daily communication to data search, from news scanning to political discussion, from sales to marketing, from shopping to auction, from stock trading to apartment renting, from banking to bill paying, from postal tracking to airline reservation, from museum browsing to trip planning, from seeking medical advice to finding love, from kids homework help to adults continuing education, from job hunting to talent search, from business advertising to personal promoting, from checking weather to checking restaurant menu, from playing games to sending greetings, from movie reviewing to music downloading, from video sharing to photo exchanging, and on and on. In a word, it helps us with everything from A to Z. It is our ultimate and 24/7 go-to place.

The Internet is powerful because it empowers all. As good education does, the Internet empowers people everywhere, in developed as well as developing world, in East as well as West. It offers the whole wide world to anyone who gets on it from anywhere on earth, a village, a classroom, a library, a home, a temple, or an Internet bar. Along the way, it carries the spirit of equality, freedom, openness, generosity, and brotherhood of the mankind. It connects the world, shrinks the world, and flattens the world, as famously said by Thomas Friedman. No other technology has reached the world so widely and so deeply. No other technology has brought the whole of mankind together so closely and so intimately. Most of all, no other technology had made the world community so equal and so similar.

That magic and power are multiplied millions of times in the land of the ancient *xiu cais* who used to know everything from their books. When go-online was all the rage in the United States in the early 1990s, there were not even many computers in China. By the end of 2006, however, China had 137 million people online. In June 2008, the Chinese netizen population reached 253 million, surpassing that of the U.S. to become the world's largest population on the Internet!

The magic and power of the Internet are also millions of times more potent and meaningful in China. After all, the Internet is not just making instant *xiu cais* out of its users. As many have observed, there is, on one hand, explosive and creative use of the Internet in China in every possible way, from chatting to blogging, from forming virtual communities to exposing local scandals, even organizing street protests. On the other, there is the ever-present government censorship, or the Great Fire Wall. Some in America described this phenomenon as a cat and mouse game and wondered how the link between the development of China's Internet and that of its democracy would work out. But I am not too worried. As another Chinese saying goes: When virtue rises one foot, vice rises ten; when vice rises ten feet, virtue rises one hundred." Virtue will win in the end.

36

What moves me most about the Internet is actually the fact that America has invented this magical and powerful technology and has shared it with the whole wide world. What grander act of internationalism, humanism and globalism could there be!?

Americans should be very proud of their homegrown and now universal Internet technology. It has not only made a dream scholar of ancient China out of everyone online from every corner of the world, it has also spread worldwide American spirit and ideals. To me, the Internet says more about American freedom and largess and says it more eloquently and practically than any American president or politicians ever have.

10. America's Lazy Drive-Throughs

Chinese saying: 懒人自有懒办法
Pronunciation: Lan Ren Zi You Lan Ban Fa
Translation: Lazy People Have Their Lazy Ways

People are innately lazy. They work because they have to, unless it is labor of love. If they could, they would stop working in a heartbeat. People have to do lots of chores, too. If they could, they would certainly ignore them. Who would want to spend hours cooking, cleaning, etc.?

But laziness could be motivation, too. If people really do not want to do something, they would find a way to have it done by other people. If they really do not want to do something in an old time- and energy-consuming way, they would find a new time- and energy-efficient way of doing it. "Lazy people have their lazy ways," as the Chinese saying goes. The best example can be seen in the United States.

The first thing that impressed me about America's lazy ways was fast food. Just combining the two concepts "fast" and "food" was enough American genius. With standardized ingredients, standardized process, standardized containers/wrappers, not to say in standardized kitchens, fast food did not require much cooking or serving, just assembling. All customers needed to do was picking a package and deciding to eat "here" or "to go."

What impressed me more than fast food was the fact that fast food was not even fast enough for Americans. They had to make it faster by adding something else, something that may very well be the most brilliant of American inventions out of laziness: the drive-through. With drive-through windows at fast food restaurants, Americans could have their fast food "on the go."

Drive-through is such a way of life in the United States that they have to be as American as McDonald's and Starbucks, if not apple pie. Besides drive-through restaurants, there are drive-through banks, drive-through dry cleaners, drive-through mailboxes, drive-through pharmacies, drive-through bill paying windows, drive-through stores, drive-through coffee kiosks, drive-through car-washes, drive-through oil changes, drive-through video returns, even drive through church services and drive-through marriage chapels!

With the surge of the Internet nowadays has come a new explosion of drive-throughs: online "drive-through" business and services! People can now order services and merchandise at these Internet drive-throughs without even having to "drive" their car "through" anywhere. How lazy, and how smart, could Americans be!?

So laziness is actually a wonderful thing. We didn't want to walk too much or too long, so we got bikes and cars. We didn't want to plow or harvest by hand all the time, so we got tractors and combines. We didn't want to buy groceries every day, so we got refrigerators. We didn't want to cook all our meals, so we got microwavable frozen dinners. We didn't want to wash clothes by hand, so we got washers and dryers. We didn't want to wash dishes by hand, either, so we got dishwashers. We didn't want to mow our lawns by hand, so we got lawn mowers. We didn't want to get up from our couch or bed to change channels on our television, so we got remote controls. (In fact, the first television remote controller made by Zenith Radio Corporation in 1950 was called, what else, Lazy Bone!) We didn't want to go to stores to shop, so we got mail order, shopping channels, and now online shopping. We didn't want, or couldn't, answer all the telephone calls, so we got answering machines. And of course, we didn't want to get out of our comfortable, safe, warm or air-conditioned cars to get any services, so we got all the drive-throughs.

Laziness is also universal, American or Chinese. A lazy person is often called a "lazy bug" in Chinese. In English, there is the famous "couch potato." But interestingly, both English and Chinese languages share one other term for lazy people: "lazybones."

By calling lazy people lazybones, speakers of both English and Chinese must have recognized the same thing: lazy people are really just lazy in their "bones," but not in their head. The laziness in their "bones" often turns into smartness in their head. The smartness in their head in turn compensates for, often many times over, the laziness in their "bones." The Chinese saying, "Lazy people have their lazy ways," no doubt has a degree of admiration in it, admiration for those who are both lazy and smart. It is often the very lazy and very smart ones among us who have come up with better ways to do things, with less time, less hassle, less energy, less materials, etc. In a word, I believe, laziness inspires humans to invent new products, services and technologies as much as necessity does. If necessity is the mother of invention, laziness must be the father. Drive-throughs are the best example.

A few years ago, as I remember, some Americans became concerned about all the drive-throughs. They complained that drive-throughs took up too much space, emitted too much pollutant air, held up traffic, etc., and campaigned to ban new drive-through businesses in some areas. But the movement didn't go very far. Americans were too lazy and too smart to abandon their drive-through lifestyle. On the contrary, their smart laziness has gone global. In 2006, McDonald's introduced the American drive-through culture into China, the fastest-growing car and fast food market.

Maybe instead of seeing it as negative, laziness should be given a positive light. Next time you call a person or child "lazybones," you might want to pause a second and imagine if that person or child would not probably invent something someday so he or she would not have to do things the expected way and change your ways, too. So just sit back, relax, and let them be, with this Chinese saying in your head: "Lazy people have their lazy ways." Or shouldn't the saying be changed to "Lazy people have their smart ways?"

☞   ☞   ☞   ☞   ☞

11. American Adoptive Parents Do Not Mind Their Children's Looks

Chinese saying: 儿不嫌母丑
Pronunciation: Er Bu Xian Mu Chou
Translation: Children Do Not Mind Their Mother's Looks

"Children do not mind their mother's looks" is a Chinese saying that describes the most natural, genuine and unconditional of human love that exists between children and their mother. It is sometimes expanded to describe one's love for one's hometown or homeland, no matter how poor or small or ugly it might be.

I was reminded of this kind of love, though in a different format, again and again by stories of Americans adopting from overseas, mostly from poor, war-torn, or disaster-stricken developing countries. I was deeply touched by the determination they have demonstrated in going through sometimes very tough and costly adoption process and the love they have shown to these adopted children, whatever their race or ethnicity might be. Therefore I would "twist" the old Chinese saying a little to show my admiration for them: American adoptive parents do not mind their children's looks.

Diversity is a trademark of the American society. In addition to belief systems and political groups of all kinds, there are as many racial and ethnic groups among Americans as there are races and ethnicities in the world. However, to live in a racially and ethnically diversified society is one thing, to have a racially and ethnically diversified family, and through adoption for that matter, is quite another. But to these adoptive American families, that seemed the most natural thing in the world.

One leading website devoted to helping people with international adoption was called Rainbow Kids. I thought that was so beautiful, fit, and remarkable a name for the site as well as for the children adopted from different countries. The founder of the website was an adoptive mother herself. With that heart-warming name for her organization, she shared with readers and future adoptive parents heart-warming experience she had had in adopting her five children from overseas.

Thousands of American couples have adopted "rainbow kids" over the last several decades. According to the Evan B. Donaldson Adoption Institute in New York, in the 30 years from 1971 to 2001, U.S. citizens adopted 265,677 children from other countries, including those of Asia, Europe, North America, South America, and Africa. According to the State Department, in 2006, for instance, the top 10 countries of origin of children adopted by Americans were China, Guatemala, Russia, South Korea, Ethiopia, Kazakhstan, Ukraine, Liberia, Colombia, and India.

Not only the race and ethnicity of these adopted children were diverse, the standards of living and health care in their birth countries were also varied, mostly low. Many of the children for adoption had been abandoned because of their health problems. But our American adoptive parents didn't mind. Some of them even chose to adopt children with health problems, even disabilities.

One adoptive family was from Boise, Idaho. The couple already had three children, two boys and one girl. But they decided to adopt another baby girl and "do something for other people, as Jesus did," they said. In an essay explaining their desire to adopt, they wrote that they had been blessed with good fortune and a loving family. But they wished to share it with a little girl in need. In need indeed, the adoption agency found a toddler in South China, a girl with a heart condition. After checking out all the medical records and seeking professional advice, they brought the little girl home to America and started her on treatment as well as a life with love and luxury she had never known or would have never known in her birth country. I could never forget the large photo in the newspaper of this Boise mother, seated, in warm orange light, looking at their youngest family addition from China asleep in her arms, a heart-felt smile bursting in her face, from ear to ear.

There were many little girl orphans in China like this one adopted in Idaho. They had been abandoned for various reasons, but mostly because of China's strict one-child family policy and the age-old Chinese belief that a family had to be carried on by a male child. The birth parents had brought these little girls into this world with more regret than love. What tragedy! Yet, bad things turn into good things, as they say in China. How could any of these little girls or anyone else had ever expected in their wildest dreams that someone from another country, of another race, speaking another language, would go through all the bureaucracy, spend months or years waiting, pay thousands of dollars of fees and expenses, fall in love with them just by looking at their photographs, travel half the world to meet them for the first time, and then bring them home to America to love, to heal, to teach, and to spoil. What love! And such tragic stories with a happy American ending have been repeated thousands upon thousands of times from China to Russia, from India to Romania, from Korea to Vietnam. This trans-racial, trans-ethnic, and trans-national love of American adoptive families has turned the most unfortunate children into the most fortunate. What magic!

For whatever reasons American adoptive parents may have had in adopting orphans from overseas, be it having no children, wishing to enlarge an existing family, or simply desiring to share their fortune with the less fortunate, as did the

44

Boise couple, their love for their adopted children has been shown not only as natural, genuine and unconditional as the love between mothers and their biological children, but also more, a lot more. If to err is human and forgive divine, I would say, to love one's biological child is human, to love an adopted child, especially a foreign child, is divine. If traditionally there was great love in children who did not mind their mother's looks, as the Chinese saying described, there is now greater love in American adoptive parents who do not mind their children's looks.

By providing a home and love to these children in need of various racial and ethnic backgrounds from around the world, American adoptive parents are not only making a rainbow of their own lives and families, or even American lives and families, they are making a rainbow of the world's lives and families.

の   の   の   の   の

12. A Separate Creation Story

Chinese saying: 自从盘古开天地
Pronunciation: Zi Cong Pan Gu Kai Tian Di
Translation: Since Pan Gu Separated Sky and Earth

One major difference between the U.S. and China is that most people in the U.S. believe in God while most people in China do not. Being an atheist in China is normal while being an atheist in America is an exception.

But of course, America is a free country and I have been pretty free to be an atheist. The only minor "irritation" may be the word "godless" that is sometimes used to describe atheists. It sounds as if atheists have "sinfully" dropped God from their life when in fact they never had God in their life in the first place. The "toughest" challenge I ever had was being asked to prove there was no God. That was after I had asked a friend if he could prove there was God. Neither of us could.

I may believe in evolution, shun any attempt by anyone to convert me, or cringe at excessive practice of faith, I am otherwise pretty comfortable living among believers. I have friends who are Christians. I have also visited churches of various denominations, at friends' invitation, to experience their art, music, atmosphere as well as services. I would blurt out "Oh my God!" from time to time. I have become used to politicians' end of speech prayer "God bless America." I also celebrate Christmas, complete with the tree and the ornaments. In a word, I am pretty OK with the mostly Christian America.

That I can feel at ease with Christianity in general may be because I see it more as a cultural phenomenon, a cultural belief, a cultural practice, and a cultural worship. One thing in particular that has made me feel that way is the Christian Bible story of Genesis, especially the Creation, Adam and Eve, etc. It reminded me of China's own legend of creation or the beginning of the world.

As the saying in the title suggests, and according to a large body of writings since the Qin times in 200s BC, it was deity Pan Gu who separated sky and earth and created the world.

As chronicled by a man called Xu Zheng of the State of Wu during the Three Kingdoms period in 200s AD, Pan Gu, a male figure, came into being in the chaos of the soup of the early universe inside a huge egg. He slept in there for 18,000 years. Upon waking up, he saw darkness all around and felt suffocated. He stretched his arms and legs, poked and kicked, and broke the egg. The soup began to gradually separate. The lighter part went up to form the sky and heavier part sank to the bottom to form the earth. For the next 18,000 years, Pan Gu kept pushing his hands up to support the sky and stomping his feet to keep the earth down. In this way, Pan Gu grew bigger and bigger, the sky grew higher and higher and the earth thicker and thicker. Finally, Pan Gu was exhausted, but created the world with his dying body. His head became East Mountain, his feet West Mountain, his torso Middle Mountain, his left arm South Mountain and his right arm North Mountain. His left eye became the sun and his right eye the moon. His hair and eyebrow became stars in the sky. His breath became wind and cloud. His voice became lightening and thundering. His flesh became the soil. His tendons and veins became roads. His bones and teeth became minerals and stones. His blood became rivers and streams. His skin and body hair became trees and plants. And his sweat became rain and dew… Then, there was the world.

Besides the separating of sky and earth, there were other Pan Gu stories. Pan Gu was not just a legendary figure; there is a mountain in Henan Province called Mt. Pan Gu, in it was a Pan Gu temple, the building materials of which are said to date back to the Han dynasty, 2,000 years ago.

Pan Gu was also only one of a pantheon of Chinese deities. In the legends of creation, there was also Nu Wa, a female figure, who created human beings out of clay, yellow clay, of course, for the yellow people the Chinese have always seen themselves as. There was Da Yu, a male figure, who led people in conquering a great flood more than 4,000 years ago.

I wonder if many Christians have ever heard of this Chinese creation story or how they responded. But they may find it interesting, as I do, that the Chinese are not religious about it. Pan Gu was never a religious figure. With the revival of traditional culture in China in recent years, there has been a new surge in Pan Gu studies and worshipping, with an annual Pan Gu festival, too. But still, to the Chinese, Pan Gu along with Nu Wa and Da Yu were part of the Chinese ancestry, folklore, history, literature, etc., but not religion. To me, Pan Gu's was a beautiful Chinese creation story, as beautiful as the Christian creation story.

Life and universe have existed for millions of years, with millions more to go. There seems to be no hurry for any religious or cultural group to settle on the origin of life or universe, the eternal mystery and the eternal quest of the mankind. We can take our time, keep an open mind, learn all the splendid and fascinating cultures and stories of our common yet diverse human family, including descendants of Adam and Eve, of Pan Gu and Nu Wa, and everyone between the sky and the earth, and enjoy the ride as well as the suspension of this life in this universe.

ぶ　ぶ　ぶ　ぶ　ぶ

13. Airing Family Shame on TV vs. Hiding Shame of SARS

Chinese saying: 家丑不可外扬
Pronunciation: Jia Chou Bu Ke Wai Yang
Translation: Family Shame Should Never Be Made Public

"Family shame should never be made public" is an age-old Chinese advice. It tells people that if there is any disgrace, embarrassment, humiliation, or scandal in their family, they should do their best to hide it from the public, forever if possible. Similar in a way to "Don't wash your dirty linen in public" in English, the Chinese saying puts more emphasis on the family than the individual.

This Chinese consciousness of shame is closely related to another Chinese concept: the concept of face. Face can mean honor, respect, prestige, etc. Saving one's face is very important in the Chinese culture. It is not just an individual matter, but a family one. A sure way to make a man and his family lose face is to have his family shame revealed.

Two occurrences over the years made me think, or re-think, about this Chinese saying and practice: the confession/therapy type talk shows in America and the SARS breakout in China.

For several seasons during the 1990s, I was hooked on the daytime talk shows. I watched whenever possible Oprah Winfrey as well as the shows of Phil Donahue, Geraldo Rivera, Sally Jesse Raphael, etc. For me, it was a great way to learn about America and Americans.

Some of the shows, however, made me a little uncomfortable. For instance, Oprah had a woman guest who was a victim of incest from age two, with her stepfather being the perpetrator. One episode of the Geraldo show featured women who married their rapists, along with a specialist on the stage providing analysis. On one of Sally's shows, a guest told the audience that he'd fathered a child with a 14-year-old girl. He was reportedly arrested afterwards. There were other shows where guests revealed their various secrets, including marital infidelity, paternity tests, homosexual tendency, transgender identity, etc.

I couldn't help thinking how awful it was for these people to tell the public, or the world, their "family shame." Shouldn't such accounts have remained on a psychiatrist's couch? Did everything have to come out of the closet? Was there no more shame left? I wished those guests, and their hosts, had known the Chinese saying about hiding one's family shame. But they were Americans, and different.

In early 2003, SARS (severe acute respiratory syndrome) broke out in parts of China and Asia. It threatened lives of people there as well as anyone who had come into contact with the people there. Also under threat was the reputation of the Chinese government.

For days and weeks, American media reported and criticized the Chinese government for covering up the outbreak, failing to provide information, issuing false assurances, even hiding patients, etc. They attributed the secrecy over SARS to the communist party's authoritarian control of the media and the society.

I felt sad, disappointed, and frustrated.

It was logical for the media to link the authoritarian nature of the communist rule with its effort to cover up an unfavorable development. It was also reasonable to compare the cover-up of SARS by the Chinese government with that of the Chernobyl accident by the Soviet Union. However, there was another aspect, a Chinese aspect, to the cover-up, as the saying "family shame should never be made public" showed. The practice of secrecy, or hiding family shame, was not only communist, but also Chinese. For the Chinese, the concept of family was not only individual, but also collective.

In fact, "nation" in written Chinese contains two characters: nation and family. An individual family was sometimes referred to as the small family while the national family the big family. If an individual's family shame should be hidden from the pubic, a nation's family shame should be all the more so. If a man could lose face in the community when his family shame was made public, a nation would lose face in the international community when the nation's family shame was made public.

It was thus both authoritarian and Chinese for the Chinese government to try to control information about SARS. In the Chinese leaders' minds, an epidemic was a great shame of China's. They wanted it hidden until they could come up with a more face-saving way to deal with it. Besides diseases, they also saw deaths and injuries from accidents, natural disasters, social upheavals, poverty, etc. as shame.

It was also this combination of shame consciousness and authoritarian rule that made the Chinese government do what they did over half a century: controlling information on the death toll of the 1960s famine resulting from the failed Great Leap Forward; declining offers of aid by international organizations after the Tangshan earthquake killed 200,000 Chinese in 1976; restricting foreign journalists from visiting regions deemed too poor in the early 1980s, or moving people temporarily into better apartments in the same period to impress their overseas relatives; and blacking out all information of the Tiananmen crackdown in 1989, and suppressing any mention of it since...

Oh. It may be culturally reflexive for an individual to hide his or her shame, or dirty linen. It was certainly politi-

51

cally convenient for an authoritarian regime to hide shameful events under its rule. But at what price, in both cases?

I thought about that woman survivor of incest, indeed a family shame. But if the abuse had not been revealed, the woman would have to continue living in the darkness of secrecy and never be able to start a new life. Her perpetrator would never have been exposed and brought to justice and her mother would never have realized that silence could mean acquiescence.

I thought about that man who admitted to fathering a child with an under-age girl, a really shameful thing to tell. But if he had not confessed, a crime would have been condoned, the violation of the girl would have gone on without redress, and the public would never have learned about a criminal walking free.

Then I thought about all similar and/or different "family shames" hidden by Chinese citizens. How many miseries, possibly crimes, must have been endured in silence.

And I thought about all the "shames" of China hidden by the Chinese government. My heart sank. It sank with pain and sympathy for all those who had lost loved ones in various disasters in China, natural or political, without any public acknowledgement or proper compensation. It also sank with disappointment and indignation at the Chinese government. By withholding, even falsifying, information regarding poverty, hunger, deaths, injuries, diseases as well as grievances, it has harmed instead of protected the Chinese people, damaged instead of earned its credit among nations, and most importantly, lost instead of gained face in the world community.

I realized that the old saying "Family shame should never be made public" was really old, outdated, and no longer a good advice in today's world.

That world, on international level, is an open, fast, connected, and interdependent global village. No nation should, or can, stay closed. No government should, or can, withhold information, shameful or not, especially concerning people's health or safety in cases such as SARS where one people are affected, all peoples are affected.

That world, on individual level, is an ever more wired community. Except for "trash" and "tabloid" kind of secrets, no one should have to suffer silently any "family shame" anymore. Tell it to friends or neighbors, schools or churches, doctors or counselors, real or virtual support groups.

By airing and sharing instead of hiding "family shame," of an individual family or a national family, one would help build a healthy and strong society and save face for us all—the human family.

᷇ ᷇ ᷇ ᷇ ᷇

Part 2. American Issues

14. Life and Death Between Pro-Life and Pro-Choice

Chinese proverb: 你死我活
Pronunciation: Ni Si Wo Huo
Translation: I Live You Die

Abortion was a common practice in China, without much debate, at least when I lived there till the end of 1980s. It was legal, encouraged, and free. To get an abortion appointment was like getting any other medical appointment. There were never "back-alley" or "clothes hanger" stories in China. On the contrary, people got in trouble for refusing an abortion and giving births outside the government-set quotas. The quotas were, of course, part of China's national family planning policy adopted since the late 1970s, which allowed married couples in urban areas to have one child only and rural couples no more than two children.

Personally, I had no problem with the policy. Interested in population issues and having read some population works, I came to realize that the higher the living standard the fewer children people had or wanted. For China, with a low living standard and a huge population, the one-child policy was simply a proactive measure to raise the living standard by slowing down the population growth rather than wait for the living standard to go up first and then have the birth rate to come down. Since the policy was designed in the interests of the whole society, therefore, all couples had a part to play. If a couple did not act responsibly, abortion became a necessary last resort in preventing un-planned births. There was, of course, resistance, especially in rural areas. But it was more a reaction to the harsh enforcement of the policy, along with administrative and financial punishment for offenses, than a dispute over the morality of abortion itself.

In the U.S., however, abortion was a totally different issue. It had nothing to do with a national population policy, or any pressure of a population explosion, or any effort to raise national living standard. It was a purely private and individual matter. Yet at the same time, it was not so private or individual, for it had become the focal point of a national debate involving politics, religion, philosophy, medicine, human rights, not to say average Americans in their millions, as women, men, couples, and voters.

But I didn't realize the seriousness of the contention between pro-life and pro-choice groups until I heard an ABC News special in the early 1990s describe it as America's "new civil war."

It did feel like a war, with tension and hostility between the two groups running high and through the media. It also looked like a war because the confrontation was not limited to verbal form only. While pro-lifers called pro-choicers baby-killers, they themselves had resorted to violence such as attacking abortion clinics and terrorizing women seeking abortion services, etc., even resulting in a number of deaths.

There seemed to be no better term to describe the situation other than *ni si wo huo*, as expressed in the Chinese proverb, or "I live and you die." Not only did it describe the fight between the pro-life and pro-choice groups, it also described the life and death of the unborn.

The root of the debate, as I came to learn, was the question of when life began. In the Roe v. Wade ruling, the Supreme Court declared that abortion in the first trimester should be a decision between the woman and her doctor. Abortion in the second trimester may be restricted but not prohibited. Only abortion in the third trimester may be regulated and even prohibited except when the life of the mother was in danger. The assumption seemed to be that life began in the third trimester of gestation or even at birth.

58

But pro-lifers believed that life began at conception or even the second an egg was released and fertilized. Their strongest argument was represented in this definition: Since death was legally classified as the absence of brain waves and a heartbeat, the opposite equaled life. An unborn child had brain waves at 41 days and heartbeat at 24 days, they pointed out. Therefore, they believed, women who used abortion pills or medication during even the first stage of their pregnancies were killing unborn babies.

Killing was pretty strong a choice of word. But pro-lifers' position did remind me that the belief of life-begins-at-conception was not a new one.

In China, for instance, there was an age-old tradition, especially in rural areas, to count a newborn's age as one-year-old. That year, of course, was actually the nine months the baby lived in the mother's womb. When a lunar new year came around, another year was added to the baby's age. The practice caused a lot of confusion among the Chinese themselves, since urban Chinese counted their age the Western way, the rural Chinese often had one extra year, sometimes two, "added" to theirs. Unfortunately, this folk belief had never become "official." I doubt it was ever a consideration in the making and enforcing of China's population policy. It was certainly not a consideration in the countless abortions sought and given in the country.

The abortion debate in the U.S. has been a real education for me. However, as a woman and a mother, a U.S. citizen with a Chinese background, understanding the Constitutional rights, especially the right to privacy as defended in Roe v. Wade, concerned of the beginning of an unborn life, appreciative of public policies for social interests, and recognizing the unequal burden on women in un-planned pregnancies, I feel fast stuck in the middle, between life and choice, American and Chinese, and social and individual.

I am not sure if a middle ground could be reached in America's life and death struggle over abortion, or the "new civil war," or how it would end. But I am sure it would be waged in China someday, too, when the focus there is no longer totally on the pressure of population growth. After all, folks there had long believed that a baby was one-year-old upon birth.

15. It Takes a Big Heart to Embrace Free Speech

Chinese proverb: 宰相肚里能撑船
Pronunciation: Zai Xiang Du Li Neng Cheng Chuan
Translation: A Great Person's Heart is Big Enough to Pole a Boat In

The proverb above is a praise of a *zai xiang*, or prime minister, named Wang Anshi of the Song Dynasty China. He was famous for his reforms. But he was also famous for his special tolerance. After the death of his wife, he took a young concubine. The young woman was not happy and got a lover. Realizing his own old age, Wang did not blame her. Instead, he gave his blessing, and silver, to the young couple and presided over their wedding on the moon festival. People were so impressed that they described his heart as big enough to pole a boat in. The proverb came to be used to recognize or encourage tolerance in all circumstances. But what made me recall this proverb?

In the late 1990s, celebrity chef Wolfgang Puck and his wife Barbara Lazaroff opened a restaurant called ObaChine in downtown Seattle. It was part of their chain business offering dishes from China, India, Japan, Korea, Malaysia and Thailand. No sooner had they opened the door than they triggered a controversy. Protesters were stationed outside; interviews were conducted on TV; letters to the editor appeared in local papers; etc. What was the matter? A poster hanging in the restaurant: a seated Chinese man in a traditional gown, with a skullcap and a long braid, holding a cup of tea, and smiling. The protesters said that the image was an insult to Asian Americans, especially the Chinese, and called the owners racist.

That was when I wondered if the protesters had ever heard of, or remembered, this Chinese proverb about having a big heart to pole a boat in.

America was such a diversified country, with people from every racial and ethnic group in the world, representing all religious and cultural groups, that Americans were bound to have different ways of doing, seeing, and understanding things. With all the differences, however, this great country allowed the highest degree of freedom, most notably freedom of speech and expression. At the same time, the law of the land also said that no one could discriminate against anyone else because of his or her race, gender, age, religion, national origin, etc. To me, that was a perfect arrangement. On the one hand, you could have all the freedom to be different. On the other, you couldn't discriminate against anyone else because he or she was different. The glue for all the differences was tolerance, or a big heart.

The level of that tolerance, or the size of the heart, obviously varied from person to person, group to group.

One typical line of the protestors' argument was that the painting was not art, because it depicted a time and a condition in the Chinese history, and it belittled the Chinese. I assumed by "time" they meant the Qing dynasty, from mid 17th to early 20th century, and by "condition" they meant the Manchu rule under which men had to wear their hair in a long braid.

But what works of art did not depict a time and condition of a people or a culture? Artists themselves lived in a time and a condition. Their art was bound to reflect, through their eyes and techniques, the time and the condition they lived in.

As a lay person, I could see art of two kinds. One was the pure kind, for the sake of beauty only, and timeless, such as traditional Chinese paintings of mountains and rivers, flowers and birds, etc. The other kind served a purpose, commercial or political, for instance, and for a specific time. The restaurant poster was a work of the second kind. Its name was "Thé de la Chine," or "Tea of China," by a French artist who had lived in the early 20th century when France was having a love affair with China and importing a lot of Oriental merchandise including tea. The work was commercial. After serving its purpose of promoting tea, the poster had become a coveted item of art collection.

The Qing dynasty may not have been the most glorious "time" and "condition" in China, with corrupt and incompetent governments, etc. But it was history. Besides, in the "time" and "condition" of that painting, the tea trade was flourishing. In today's terms, the tea trade then between China and Europe must have created a lot of jobs and income for Chinese tea farmers and tea traders. How could a historical poster promoting tea trade be racial?

The poster story, however, was not the only political controversy involving art that I followed in those days.

National Review, a political opinion magazine, once used a cartoon for its cover story "China syndrome." The article was about the Clinton Administration's alleged China connections in campaign financing. The cartoon showed a President Clinton wearing a southern Chinese peasant hat and holding a tea tray, a Hillary in the outfit of a Chinese Red Guard of the 1960s and holding a Little Red Book of Mao, and an Al Gore in a maroon monk robe and holding a pot for donations. I thought it was fun.

A number of Asian-American organizations, however, didn't think so. They protested and boycotted the magazine, claiming that the cartoon was an insult to Chinese Americans because it showed buckteeth, etc. So? It was a political cartoon and was supposed to caricature. If someone had to have a hard time taking it, shouldn't it have been the Clintons and Gore?

To me, both the poster and the cartoon controversies seemed to be a case where a little more tolerance, or a bigger heart, was needed to let others enjoy free speech and expression as we did ourselves.

There are many things in our life we may not like very much. There are also people we may not choose to associate with. It is all natural and human. As long as they are not in violation of any law, why shouldn't we let them be? Everything does not have to fit in a standard of "political correctness." If it did, it would be like the Great Proletarian Cultural Revolution in China in the 1960s-70s that I lived through, when everything had to conform to Mao's teachings in letter and in spirit. Otherwise, they had to be smashed.

Think about it. With a big heart, those ObaChine poster protestors would not only have seen the image of a traditional Chinese man peddling tea, they would have also seen the fact that the Chinese/Asian cuisines were so popular in America that the non-Chinese/Asian owners felt interested and encouraged enough to have started a chain serving them in the first place. They would have also seen the fact that the restaurant chain had hundreds of employees of all ethnic and racial backgrounds working in various cities. Similarly, with a big heart, those National Review cartoon protestors would not only have seen the less than beautiful buckteeth or the image of the ultra-left Red Guard. They would have also seen the reach of China's growing influence in American life, not just economic, but also political, actual or perceived.

The restaurant was closed later on, for various reasons, with the poster controversy as a factor. The chain reportedly had similar paintings in its L.A. and Phoenix locations, without controversy. I wondered why.

Years later, during a trip to Alaska, I spotted an identical poster on an old Chinese teahouse in Fairbanks. It was such a delight, even joy, to see it; I could almost feel the warmth of

"Thé de la Chine" in that remotest and coldest part of America.

But no one else noticed. It was just an old painting, after all.

❧ ❧ ❧ ❧ ❧

16. Affirmative Action in America and China

Chinese saying: 老中青三结合
Pronunciation: Lao Zhong Qing San Jie He
Translation: Three-Way Combination of the Old,
the Middle-Aged and the Young

The "Three-way combination of the old, the middle-aged and the young" was the abbreviation of a government personnel policy in China during the 1960s and 1970s. It served as a guideline for government bodies at various levels in the appointment of their high officeholders. The policy required that all three groups—the old, the middle aged and the young—be represented in leadership positions. It was later expanded to a five-way combination to include women and minorities. Like a quota system, the "combination" was an effort to make the government look like the population. It was just one of many practices during the Cultural Revolution under the slogan "Politics in Command," meaning everything had to follow the correct political ideology.

I had no idea, until after I came here, that the United States practiced "political correctness," too, and even had a quota system called "affirmative action" designed to improve the status of the minorities. I didn't know how race played out in everyday life in America, either, since race was not an issue in the racially homogeneous China.

One lesson on race came to me in the process of a few job applications I had attempted. In the application forms, the applicant was asked to check one of a number of boxes indicating various racial and ethnic groups. I had no problem finding my box, of course. But I was amazed that now in

America I was not only Chinese and Asian, I was also Asian-Pacific!

It was hard to describe the exact feeling I had while checking the boxes, as it was something I had never done before in my life. Was I supposed to expect some kind of preference in the job application? Or was I trying to show the potential employer my pride as an Asian applicant? Or was I just providing information for someone compiling ethnic statistics for the government? I couldn't say I enjoyed the experience. But it didn't really matter because I never got those jobs.

As an Asian immigrant, I had been basically a neutral bystander over the mostly black and white race issue in America. That was the case until the start in 1998 of a heated debate over Initiative 200 in Washington state where I was a resident. The initiative was to stop affirmative action, or "racial quotas," in all government programs. It gave me a good opportunity to learn and think about the issue, and to later come to my own answer to this question: Which one was fairer, affirmative action or Initiative 200?

While Title VI of the Civil Rights Act of 1964 declared that "No person in the United States shall, on the ground of race, color, or national origin, be excluded from participation in, be denied the benefits of, or be subjected to discrimination under any program or activity receiving federal financial assistance," Washington state's Initiative 200 read that "The state shall not discriminate against, or grant preferential treatment to, any individual or group on the basis of race, sex, color, ethnicity, or national origin in the operation of public employment, public education, or public contracting."

The two statements had similar wordings, but their emphasis was different. The federal one emphasized the protection of individuals from discrimination, while the Washington state one emphasized the protection of the wider population from preferential treatment to individuals. Initiative 200, as expected, passed. Even as a "new comer," I could see why, in three ways.

One. Affirmative action was a policy to correct past mistakes by overdoing something positive. But since everything, except time and space, was limited, overdoing could also be overstepping. When preferences were given to one group or another in college admissions, job offers, contract awards, etc. to enhance their opportunities, the rights to equal opportunities of others had to be affected. The practice may be justice to one American but not to another who was also or more qualified but had to lose out because of historical issues not of his or her own fault.

Two. Affirmative action was a policy to promote fair representation of the population in American public life. But fairness was in the eye of the beholder. For instance, while supporters of affirmative action talked about the under representation of blacks and Hispanics on American campuses, they also believed that Asians were over-represented. That may have been, academically. However, they didn't seem to notice the under- or zero- representation of Asians in college basketball, for instance, which was dominated by blacks. If it had been necessary to adjust entrance requirements to improve black and Hispanic representation in higher learning, shouldn't the similar have been considered to increase Asian representation in college basketball?

Three. Affirmative action was meant to compensate for disadvantages suffered by the minority groups. But since disadvantages were hard to measure or compare across the groups, compensations would be hard to determine. For blacks, supporters suggested that affirmative action should be in place for as long as there had been slavery. But there were more disadvantaged groups than blacks. How would they determine the compensations for other groups, including women, Native Americans, Hispanic Americans, Asian Americans, etc., especially immigrants, if they could measure their disadvantages?

Over the last few decades, most immigrants like me to settle in the United States came from Asia, the former Soviet Union and East Europe. Except for a few with investment capacity or special skills, most didn't have money, didn't speak English, didn't know how American system worked, didn't have a job waiting, etc. Most importantly, many immigrants themselves, not their forefathers, had lived under totalitarian systems, had never had freedom of speech, freedom of religion, even freedom to choose a job or to travel. Many had also suffered political persecutions or ravages of war. But that seemed to lead to a wrong question: Were these immigrants more disadvantaged or less than America's native minorities?

However, it might have been an "advantage" that the immigrants did not have any knowledge of America's affirmative action upon arriving in the United States. They didn't expect any special treatment for their ethnic or racial background. Most of them had learned long ago that America was the land of freedom and equality. When they came, they were already prepared to start anew, to compete with other Americans, and to make the best of the equal opportunities America had to offer.

The affirmative action in America was certainly different from the "Three-way combination" policy in China of the Cultural Revolution years. But the former did remind me of the latter, especially with their similar emphasis on making the government or colleges look like the population.

I would have voted for Initiative 200 if I had been a citizen then. I would have also voted for any initiative that would do away with the "trouble," or troubled feelings, checking those racial or ethnic identification boxes on a form. No one should have to check those boxes when he or she applies for a job or college, especially in the United States of America where, as Dr. Martin Luther King, Jr., had dreamed, people should be judged by the content of their character, not the color of their skin.

17. The Divisive Classifying of Asian Americans

Chinese proverb: 分而治之
Pronunciation: Fen Er Zhi Zhi
Translation: Divide and Rule

First of all, to avoid any misunderstanding, I proudly and positively announce here that I am an American citizen of Chinese ethnicity. However, it is one thing when I choose to tell my race and ethnicity, it is another when I was required to tell while other Americans were not. I am talking about Census 2000.

The Census 2000 form, the short form I received at least, was confusing and illogic in terms of race and ethnicity. It asked first if I was Spanish/Hispanic/Latino, and then if I was White, Black, American Indian, or Alaska Native. Those were all broad racial classifications, of course. Since I was none of the above, I was asked to check one of the specific boxes listing various Asian ethnicities including Asian Indian, Chinese, Filipino, Japanese, Korean, Vietnamese, other Asian, followed by Native Hawaiian, Guamanian or Chamorro, Samoan, and Other Pacific Islander.

But why did the government have to know if an Asian American was of Chinese or Korean ethnicity, for instance, but not if a European American was of English or German ethnicity, or if an African American Ethiopian or Somalian, or if a Hispanic American Cuban or Mexican?

It so happened that a roundtable on race relations was being held in town. The panel consisted of members of an organization devoted to the development of leadership in Asian Pacific Americans, or APAs. As I found out, it was the APA community that had initiated the effort to have the ethnic classification of Asian Americans adopted in Census 2000. This group was among those behind the initiative. I really took my questions to the right people.

A woman panelist, who was also a faculty member of a university in California, started answering my questions by saying that because Asian Americans were all different, etc. A lady in the audience cut in, echoing her, "We are all different. We cannot be lumped together as just Asian Americans." A gentleman then took over, emphasizing every word; "We want to tell that we are different. We want to be positive about who we are. We want to show that we are here to stay..." But were European Americans not positive about themselves, I asked. Someone shouted from the audience, "They don't need to be. Because they've always been here!" But what about African Americans, Hispanic Americans, I added. There was a pause. Then somebody mumbled, "They have their problems." "We have to take care of ourselves," another voice said. The Q&A session turned into an education session for me, as if I did not feel positive about my racial/ethnic identity, when in fact I felt exactly the other way around.

There was a strong sense in the room that day that APAs were still very much considered foreign in America. In the executive summary of a newly published book by this group, there was even a section under Racial Identities called "APAs as Permanent Aliens in American Culture." As a matter of fact, an APA friend of mine came up with a new term of his own: "Americanized Alien." To further illustrate the point, a retired gentleman in the audience stood up and told a story from his earlier years. He and his wife, both APAs, had been in a supermarket one day. Someone was collecting signatures in the store for a ballot issue. The person went up and down the aisles to various shoppers, all white, for their signatures, but walked right past the Asian couple.

I didn't "rebut" him then. But I had an exactly opposite experience. As someone who wanted to learn about Ameri-

71

can politics, I had just been to a political party picnic. A gentleman, white for the "census" purpose here, holding some pamphlets and a signature pad, walked up to me, explained his cause, and asked for my support and signature. I was pleased to be asked but had to explain to him that I was not citizen yet, though I was a citizen-to-be. He smiled, said welcome to my coming citizenship, and then walked on to other people.

So while that gentleman in the audience believed that he was still seen as foreign even though he was citizen and I was mistaken for a citizen when I was really still foreign, we were missing the point, which was: What was the point having Asian Americans check their specific ethnic identity on the census form?

I had more questions. By this kind of ethnic classifying, were we Asian Americans not making ourselves more different than same and more foreign than American? If this was for government funding, were we not pitching one ethnic or racial group against another when most minority communities had similar needs? If this was an effort of affirmative action, why wasn't the same method used also for African Americans, Hispanic Americans, etc.? If this was a tool to promote good citizenship, how would a Chinese or a Korean identification help do just that? If this was a way to help the government or fellow Americans tell a Chinese American from a Korean American, then why wasn't the same also done to tell an English American from a German American, or an Ethiopian American from a Somalian American, or a Cuban American from a Mexican American?

The group at the roundtable and others like it must have worked hard to achieve the special ethnic classification treatment for Asian Pacific Americans in Census 2000. They seemed to believe that there was power in being counted differently than all other Americans. But I begged to disagree.

72

In their belief, there seemed to be a degree of Asian cen-teredness. The panel as well as the audience emphasized time and again that the classification was necessary for the interests of APAs as a minority group. But there were so many other minorities in America. Yet no other groups were "equally" classified in the census. There was also no known effort by the APAs to coordinate with other minority groups in Amer-ica in achieving the same "status" in the census.

In their belief, there also seemed to be a degree of self-denial of American-ness. What occurred to me as striking was that most APAs in that audience were genuine Americans. They spoke flawless and accent-free American English, which told of at least more than one generation living in America. Yet, they still felt themselves more foreign than American. They seemed to dwell on how different they were and spoke of APAs as "we" or "us" and the rest of America as "they" or "them."

But most of all, their belief reminded me of the Chinese proverb in the title: "Divide and rule," except in a reversed way. Reversed because the proverb was an advice from a ruler's point of view, that it was easier to rule a people by di-viding it. What it implied was that to be strong, a people had to be united. It was therefore only logical that as a minority group, Asian Pacific Americans would be stronger if they acted as one big united group, pan-Asian American, if you like, rather than as many ethnic sub-groups. Yet it was the APAs who wanted to divide and sub-divide themselves, not against a ruler, but against the rest of America.

I had no doubt that those APA groups behind the ethnic classification in Census 2000 had noble intentions, with the interests of the community at heart. But it was possible that their good intentions might have brought not so good result: making Asian and Pacific Americans stay their ethnic-selves, different, foreign, and less American longer than necessary.

Why not "lump" APAs together as "just" Asian Americans? After all, divided, you are weak; united, you are strong.

18. Judging Mulan with Political Correctness?

Chinese saying: 古为今用
Pronunciation: Gu Wei Jin Yong
Translation: Making the Past Serve the Present

It was such an excitement when Disney opened the summer 1998 season with a blockbuster, Mulan, the cartoon movie based on the Chinese story of a girl soldier. I applauded Disney for embracing world culture and introducing it to American children, and children everywhere.

But the excitement turned into bewilderment when I learned some of the comments about the movie. One father, for instance, told me that he had taken his family to see it but was bothered by the fact that Mulan had to "cross-dress" in order to fight as a soldier in battles. He was not alone. Similar sentiments were expressed in newspaper and online opinions. Some critics even pointed out that the movie was sending a wrong message to impressionable youth. What was the wrong message? It was that Mulan could succeed only in a traditional male role.

That was incredible, incredible that anyone would judge a movie character from an ancient time and an ancient country with the political correctness of the late 20th century America.

The story "Mulan joins the army" is well known in China. It was first recorded in a poem dated to 500s AD and had been passed on since in various forms. Mulan's hometown was said to be in Henan province, in central China. Her father was too ill when the draft paper for his military service came from the emperor. So Mulan disguised herself as a man and joined the military in her father's place. She did it for her father and her family, not to "succeed" in a woman's or a man's role.

But imagine, if Mulan really had to be judged with today's political correctness, how many more "wrong" messages the movie could have sent, and how many questions it could have raised?

For instance, was it not "wrong" that the emperor was not democratically elected? Did he have the authority to conscript men to fight? Were gay men allowed to serve in the ancient Chinese army? Wasn't it wrong that Mulan's parents tried to arrange a marriage for her through a matchmaker instead of letting Mulan choose her own love? Wasn't it discrimination that women were not recruited to fight alongside men in combat? Shouldn't Mulan have organized an initiative demanding the right for women of the ancient country to join the army? Or better, wasn't it illegal for the invaders to attack Mulan's homeland in the first place? Shouldn't there have been a world organization to condemn the invading country in a security council or send a peacekeeping force to China? These assumptions were, of course, ridiculous.

Mao Zedong, China's long time leader, had a famous policy phrase regarding the study of China's history: "Making the past serve the present." What he meant was that history shouldn't be studied for the sake of study only. It should be utilized to serve modern China. The idea was certainly good. The past always offered lessons for the present. However, Mao, erudite in Chinese history and classics, developed the idea into a high political art. He brilliantly made use of Chinese historical figures and events to insinuate doubts, criticism and attacks against rivals, critics and dissidents in the party, especially during the Cultural Revolution. He launched campaigns simultaneously criticizing, for instance, ancient figures of China and party figures of the day. The best example was the Campaign of Criticism of Confucius and Lin Biao, once his designated successor.

Critics of Mulan may have never heard of Mao's policy, but their views of the ancient character did remind me of how past had been used for the convenience of modern day politics.

If, in view of the politically correct, Mulan shouldn't have had to dress like a man in order to fight in the military, then many Disney movie stories would also have to be changed. For instance, Pocahontas shouldn't have fallen in love with an English colonist whose people had invaded her land. She should hate the enemy. Cinderella shouldn't have dreamt of a miracle that would turn her from a maid into a princess. She should work for it. Snow White shouldn't have waited for some prince charming to rescue her. She should be an independent woman and save herself.

Political correctness may be practiced in America today, but its heyday was in China during its Cultural Revolution years. The great irony was that Mulan was also criticized in her own country. The ultra-leftists believed that Mulan didn't start out with a consciousness to fight for her country. She did it in the interests of her father and her family. Therefore, they deemed her too narrow- and too family-minded to meet modern China's political correctness where the interests of the party and the country always came first.

One thing critics of Mulan, in the U.S. or China, failed to see was that historical figures lived in different times and circumstances. Their words and deeds were the result of their times and circumstances. We could always choose to learn from the positive aspects of the past, and not judge historical figures by the political understanding, or correctness, of today's America or China.

With an objective attitude, we could see that there was a lot our children could learn from historical figures, even those in fairy tales: From Pocahontas, for instance, they could learn that love and understanding do conquer obstacles, between individuals, tribes, or nations. From Cinderella, they could

77

learn that one should try to endure hardship when necessary while hoping and working for the better. From Snow White, they could learn that one should always keep dreams alive, girls or boys, because dreams could really come true. From Mulan, of course, they could learn that women could do as well as, or better than, men if they had courage and determination.

After all, Mulan was as tough as a man in military battles, as filial as any daughter before her parents, and as feminine as any woman in domestic life. How could her story be sending any wrong message? To me, she was an ancient model of the modern day women's lib.

Disney did a truly superb job with Mulan the movie, from the clever adaptation of the Chinese story to the excellent animation, etc. What was more significant was that by transforming the "past" from around the world into popular cartoon movies of the "present," especially the positive past for a positive present, Disney has helped improve not only America's present, but also the world's present. That is what "Making the past serve the present" should be all about.

ॐ   ॐ   ॐ   ॐ   ॐ

19. The Most Admired, or Un-admired, Man of 1998

Chinese saying: 山中无老虎，猴子称大王
Pronunciation: Shan Zhong Wu Lao Hu, Hou Zi Cheng Da Wang
Translation: When the Tiger Is Away from the Mountain, the Monkey Proclaims Himself King

Gallup Poll did again in 1998 as they had done every year since 1948, asking Americans to name their most admired man of the year. Surprisingly or not surprisingly, the most admired man of that year was... President Bill Clinton!?

The choice was totally beyond me. Immediately, the Chinese saying in the title came to me: When the tiger is away from the mountain, the monkey proclaims himself king. What the saying meant that was when real heroes were not around, the lesser heroes would take their place. I couldn't believe it. Who were those folks that had been polled? Where had they been?

Bill Clinton, if the folks had followed any news, became the second president in 1998 to be impeached in American history, with Andrew Johnson being the first back in 1867. A married man and a father, Clinton first disgraced the White House and the First Family with his liaison with an intern. He then debased the presidency by lying to the American people about the affair. He again dishonored the justice system he had sworn twice to uphold and defend by attempting to cover up the mess. For his immoral and un-presidential conduct, he was impeached on two charges: perjury and obstruction of justice.

Even though for various reasons votes in the Senate fell short to convict and remove Clinton from office, the fact that

79

he was impeached because of the scandal, that he admitted to the nation on television his improper relationship with the young woman, and that the details of his affair were broadcast on the World Wide Web, was enough shame for any man for life, not to say for any year. In another word, Clinton lost face in the biggest, highest and widest possible way. How on earth could anyone vote him the most admired man, rather than the most un-admired man, of the year?

I tried to understand how Clinton could still be admired after such a disgrace.

People must have felt that Clinton had done a good job as a president. That may be so in various ways. But a president does not make policy decisions totally by himself. He relies on the advice of professionals and experts. President Clinton, for instance, won the 1996 re-election by relying heavily on the advice of one top consultant, confidant and friend, and by shifting his position to the center and towards the right. He also, more than any other president, relied on the polls. Besides, for any bill to become law, it has to be approved and passed by the Congress. After all, America had rule of law, not of men, certainly not one man. It may be true that without Clinton, America may not have been exactly where it was in the late 1990s. It was equally true that without Clinton, America would have been spared the humiliation of having the whole world read about the infamous stains on a blue dress. Clinton could very well have been the most admired man of 1996, 1997, but definitely not 1998.

So who was the tiger, or the real hero, of that year?

To me the most admired man of any year should be someone who has achieved within that year the most in a field with the utmost effort, talent, and perseverance among us all, not necessarily one in a most powerful office.

My choice for the most admired man of 1998 was Daniel Tsui. Born in a poor peasant home in central China in 1939, Daniel looked after family cows as a boy. Later, the family managed to send him to school in Hong Kong where he excelled. From there, Tsui came to America and went on to receive his doctorate in physics from the University of Chicago in 1968. For years after that, he worked quietly, diligently and brilliantly, from Bell Labs to Princeton University. In 1998, Tsui's hard work paid off when he received the highest recognition and honor in his field, the Nobel Prize for physics, together with two fellow American scientists. From a peasant boy to a Nobel laureate? Who wouldn't admire him?

John Glenn, astronaut and politician, would have been another great candidate for the most admired man that year, with his literally out-of-this-world flight aboard the space shuttle Discovery, his second time in space, at a ripe age of over 70.

Baseball legend Mark McGwire would have qualified, too, for achieving the unachievable--setting the single-season home run record by hitting 70--not just for himself, but for the whole ever young and ever strong baby-boomer generation.

Steve Case of America Online would have also be on my short list for bringing his internet service provider company to new fame and scale that year, even with a Hollywood movie named after the AOL voice message "You've got mail!" that greeted millions of its members every day.

In the same light, the most admired man that year could also be Jeff Bezos, Seattle's local hero, who made his 4-year-old trailblazing online retailing business Amazon.com the hottest item on the stock market, and made himself as a new billionaire, not to say providing millions of customers a new and convenient way of shopping.

Any of these men would have been a better choice for the most admired man of 1998 than President Clinton. For each of them was a tiger, a real hero, instead of a monkey, a lesser one.

20. American Gun Rights Activists' Fossil Thinking

Chinese saying: 花岗岩脑袋
Pronunciation: Hua Gang Yan Nao Dai
Translation: A Granite-Like Skull

One thing I learned living in the United States was, with a degree of fear, that guns were a big part of life. It was sometimes mentioned as one of the three most important issues in an election season, as in "God, guns and gays."

Gun issue was important because it was one of life-and-death in American streets. From school shootings to mall shootings, from random sniper shootings to shoot-outs with police, from lonely teenagers seeking attention to disgruntled employees taking revenge, from crying students and parents huddled in a schoolyard to dazed mall shoppers describing the horror in a parking lot, gun crime stories and images have been a staple in American life.

According to the U.S. Bureau of Alcohol, Tobacco and Firearms, there were, in 1999, about 200 million guns in private ownership in the United States, from single-shot rifles to sophisticated and deadly assault weapons. Every year, according to the National Rifle Association, the ownership would grow by 4.5 million. In 2004, according to General Social Survey, 36.5% of Americans reported having a gun in their home. That's two out of five American homes.

Those guns did not just stay in a drawer or cabinet. Of America's already higher rate of homicide than that of other developed countries, firearms were used to commit 68% of the 14,860 homicides in the U.S. in 2005, according to Federal Bureau of Investigation. In an interview with the *New*

York Times in April 2007 after the Virginia Tech massacre, Marian Wright Edelman, president of the Children's Defense Fund, said that eight American children and teenagers were lost to gun violence each day, and well over a million people had been killed by firearms in America since the murders of Robert Kennedy and the Rev. Martin Luther King Jr. in 1968.

Amidst all these grim gun tragedies and statistics, America's gun rights activists have insisted that it was people who killed, not guns. But as the Brady Campaign to Prevent Gun Violence pointed out eloquently, horrific mass killings could not have been committed with knives or baseball bats or bare fists.

It is understandable that Americans should uphold their Constitutional rights, including those written in the Second Amendment regarding firearms. But gun rights activists have almost become fundamentalistic about the Second Amendment. Their knee-jerk reaction to any further gun control effort was that it would chip away at the Second Amendment rights. I remember clearly the image on television of the late Charlton Heston, as the president of National Rifle Association, raising a rifle and shouting "From my cold and dead hands" to anyone who would challenge his Second Amendment rights.

It is true that the Second Amendment of the U.S. Constitution guarantees people's right to own and use guns. As the text goes, "A well regulated Militia, being necessary to the security of a free State, the right of the people to keep and bear Arms, shall not be infringed." But the amendment was created in 1789, more than 200 years ago, in the early stage of the nation. Regulated militia and the right to bear arms were the result of a compromise between the Federalists and the Anti-Federalists, serving to balance the power between the federal and state governments and between a federal standing army and state militias.

83

Now, more than two hundred years later, is there still the same need for a "well regulated Militia" and for Americans to "bear Arms" as then? Even Elizabeth Dole, one-time Republican presidential candidate, once said during her campaign, "You don't need an AK-47 to defend your family in modern America!" She was right. We live in modern America now, not the frontier America when one needed a gun just to survive the day and when there was a potential conflict between a federal army and the people. Do we really need to bear arms in our daily life in this Internet age as we did 200 years ago? Do we still need to be ready with our firearms so we would not be overpowered by the United States armed forces?

Things change. Society evolves. Nothing stands still. If the Constitution could be amended according to a young America's special needs then, why can't an amendment be reviewed according to a mature America's modern circumstances today? If the Constitution had been considered untouchable, or un-amendable back then, there wouldn't have even been a Bill of Rights, including the Second Amendment. To me, those who defend the Second Amendment blindly to the letter in total disregard of the changes in America over the two centuries and America's reality today can really be called gun-rights fundamentalists. The best description of them is having "a granite-like skull," as the Chinese saying in the title suggests, meaning with a fossil-like thinking.

Our granite-skull friends argued cleverly that more people should own guns and more students should carry guns to school. They believed that if more people and more students had guns with them, they could have defended themselves better in a school shooting or a mall shooting. Following their logic, maximum security would be achieved when every American, adult, teenager, man and woman, owns a gun and carries it every day, to work, to school, to supermarket, to freeways. Would everyone feel safe then? I doubt it. Carrying a gun could give one a sense of power over others without a gun. But if everybody carried a gun, no one would feel safe knowing that everybody else was also carrying a gun. Besides, wouldn't a shooting war start easily over any outbreak of anger, dispute, frustration, resentment, revenge, etc. anywhere in the country on any given day?

Our granite-skull friends also argued fallaciously that cars kill, too, and have killed more people and therefore there should be car control, too. But this one was close to nonsense. Following their theory, not only do cars kill, so do airplanes, trains, boats, bikes, etc. Not only do transportation vehicles kill, so do fire, water, electricity, natural gas, etc. Let's not stop there. What about sports equipment, toys, kitchen utensils, etc.? But there is a difference between day and night there. Cars or sports equipment are not meant to kill. Guns are. Guns are specifically and exclusively designed, built and used to kill humans and/or animals. They are not just another consumer product. They are firearms. They are weapons. They are killing devices. Therefore, they have to be treated differently from any other products.

No matter how gun rights activists have tried to deny it, gun ownership has been found positively correlated with gun crimes. One does not hear any school shootings from China because private ownership of guns is prohibited there. One does not hear any mall shootings from Japan, either, because it has the most stringent gun controls in the developed world. We do not hear many shooting crimes from England or Australia either because firearms are strictly controlled in those countries, too. When would our granite-skull-gun-rights-fundamentalist friends see the light?

The massacre by one lone gunman at Virginia Tech in early 2007 sounded the alarm once more to the seriousness of America's gun crimes and reminded us once again of the urgent need for stricter gun control. At stake were not the "cold and dead hands" of gun rights activists, but 32 cold and dead bodies of the students and teachers as well as hundreds and thousands of other innocent Americans as gun crime victims and victims to be.

The Supreme Court did rule on a landmark gun rights case in June 2008. But the 5-4 ruling, in striking down a local gun ban, only reiterated what had been understood or believed all along: the Second Amendment right was an individual right for Americans to bear arms. There were, noticeably, four justices in dissent in this ruling. I would hope, and wait, to see the dissent become majority next time.

21. America's Big Labor vs. Chinese Workers

Chinese proverb: 将心比心
Pronunciation: Jiang Xin Bi Xin
Translation: Compare Others' Heart with Your Own

Translated literally, the above Chinese proverb says comparing heart with heart. Expanded, it says comparing others' heart with your own. What it suggests is that one should be able to compare how others feel with how one feels under similar circumstances. The meaning is close to English proverb "putting yourself in another person's shoes." But what made me think of this proverb about comparing hearts?

Once upon a time, workers everywhere were brothers in solidarity. The old slogan, "Workers of the world unite!" said it all. Not only were workers able to "compare hearts" with each other and support each other, workers' unions were also natural allies of communist parties. They shared a common struggle against the capitalist class and capitalist exploitation as well as a common goal for a better life and a better world.

That of course, was a socialist belief. I knew very well that it didn't apply much in the United States. American workers, for instance, did not celebrate May Day, the International Workers Day, even though they themselves had started the holiday by commemorating the Haymarket riot in Chicago in 1886. American unions also seemed to be working out well, or coexisting well, with American businesses. But they were still unions, still representing workers, still able to understand, if not "compare hearts" with, workers elsewhere, right? Wrong. My hopes were dashed when I saw them, as "big labor," in action.

On April 12, 2000, AFL-CIO President John Sweeney along with Teamsters President James Hoffa and 10,000 labor activists gathered around the U.S. Capitol. With raised fists and voices, they were putting on their largest demonstration to date. What were they demonstrating about? They were protesting a newly signed trade deal: the U.S.-China Bilateral WTO (World Trade Organization) Agreement.

What was their message on a beautiful spring day like that? Here is a sample: "Let's keep China on probation." "Let's go to the Hill and let's give them hell." "No free people, no free trade, screw Beijing, stuff the WTO."

But it was not just Beijing they wanted to screw or China's WTO membership they wanted to stuff; they had also been in Seattle a few months earlier to protest the WTO itself and globalization in general during a WTO ministerial session there.

American labor leaders had probably never heard of the Chinese proverb "compare others' heart with your own," but I wished they had. For little did they know, while they were protesting in Washington DC and Washington state, the Chinese workers had been protesting all over China, too.

As reported in the Washington Post that same April, and according to China's Ministry of Labor and Social Security, the number of labor disputes in China in 1999 alone skyrocketed to 120,000, an average of more than 300 a day. The disputes ran from contractual disagreement to inadequate compensations to unpaid pensions to poor working conditions to management fraud.

Why was the surge of labor unrest?

As China's Ministry of Labor and Social Security estimated in March 2000, 11.74 million workers in China were to be laid off by the end of that year. In a November 1999 report, the United Nations Development Program suggested that urban unemployment in China was about to hit a new high of 18 million in 2000. Another study published in *Asiaweek* in 2001 said, between 1990 and 1999, 35 million people in China had lost their jobs.

Why was the tidal wave of layoffs?

China's economic reforms had been going on since 1978 when the country first opened up to foreign capital, technology and management. In 1997, the Chinese government made a strategic decision to privatize the bulk of China's state-owned-enterprises (SOEs), the backbone of China's once socialist economy. Of the total of 100,000 SOEs, only 1,000 of them were to be retained by the state and transformed into modern conglomerates. The rest were being merged, sold or closed. It was in that process that millions of jobs were being shed.

It may not have been easy for American unions to grasp, but China was undergoing an unprecedented transformation. While their country went from a command economy to a market-oriented economy, Chinese workers went from a "cradle to grave" welfare system to a fledgling social security and unemployment program.

While domestic effort was the more important part, the success of China's reforms also needed an encouraging environment, including the international community's support of China's membership of the WTO. Not only would the membership help further China's new market economy by increasing China's trade with the rest of the world, it would also bring more job opportunities, thus a better life, to Chinese workers.

It was, therefore, quite puzzling that as a leading workers' organization that called itself "a federation of international labor unions," the AFL-CIO opposed the WTO membership for China, which would benefit Chinese workers. It was more puzzling that as "big labor" that was supposedly on the left and opposite "big business" that was on the right, the AFL-CIO had come to be on the same side as conservatives like Patrick Buchanan in opposing China's WTO membership as well as globalization in general. How could that be?

It turned out that, according Paul Buhle, an expert on American labor, the AFL-CIO had long embraced capitalism and sought cooperation with big corporations. John Sweeney, its president, for instance, told corporate CEOs in late 1990s that AFL-CIO wanted to help American business compete in the world and create new wealth for their shareholders and employees, and to work with businesses to bake a larger pie, not just argue with them about how to divide the existing pie.

It also turned out that the AFL-CIO, along with several mostly right-wing institutes, had been a major recipient of grants from a quasi U.S. government agency. That agency, as an arm of U.S. foreign policy, had as its mission "strengthening democratic institutions around the world through non-governmental efforts" and gave support to selected political organizations, including unions, and opposition parties in foreign countries.

It then turned out that, as one of the hardest facts to learn, the AFL, founded in 1886, had also supported one of the most notorious laws in American history, namely the Chinese Exclusion Act of 1882. In 1901, as an extension of the Act was coming to an end, it lobbied Congress for reauthorization of the act. The AFL and then the AFL-CIO has also supported anti-communist policies in the U.S. since the 1950s and worked to establish non-communist and pro-American unions around the world.

With that kind of history and background, I came to see why the AFL-CIO along with the Teamsters demonstrated against the WTO agreement with China.

But China is very different now, as many have seen. By developing market economy, expanding private sector and protecting private ownership, China is not really communist any more. By switching from the dead-end state-owned-enterprises of yesterday to the trail-blazing private enterprises of today, Chinese workers also have more in common with American workers than ever.

With the vast differences between the U.S. and China, however, it would take time and effort for American workers to be able to "compare hearts" with Chinese workers. But the ever expanding trade, manufacturing, and services connecting the two countries have made it necessary for American unions to reach out to Chinese unions.

Reach out indeed, and breakthrough, too. In May 2007, a delegation headed by Teamsters leader James Hoffa arrived in China and met with the All-China Federation of Trade Unions, China's official union with 100 million members, thus ending the decades-old boycott of China by American unions. The AFL-CIO head John Sweeney was reportedly thinking of his own trip there.

With that encouraging development, I had my hopes up again: one of these days, American workers would be able to "compare hearts" with Chinese workers, and vice-versa.

ᕧ   ᕧ   ᕧ   ᕧ   ᕧ

22. Water, Entropy, WTO, and Jobs

Chinese saying: 人往高处走, 水往低处流
Pronunciation: Ren Wang Gao Chu Zou, Shui Wang Di Chu Liu
Translation: People Go Up and Water Goes Down

This Chinese saying "People go up and water goes down" states a fact of life, of human nature as well as Mother Nature. Water flows down from a higher surface to a lower surface, but never the other way round. People move up from a lower level to a higher level in education or age, but never the other way round. The saying is a universal truth. It is both simple and highly scientific. I am thinking of entropy.

Entropy is the name of the state of microscopic disorder in nature. It is the central concept of the second law of thermodynamics. The general idea of the law is that entropy always increases and does not spontaneously decrease. In other words, thermal energy always flows from the hot to the cold reservoir, from being localized to being dispersed, but never the other way round.

Although entropy is the process of change of energy from order to disorder, I am intrigued by it with its one-way movement, just like water, and its irreversibility. Although entropy is a theory in physical science, I am intrigued by its existence, as I see it, in human, social, economic, and technological development, in a positive way, of course.

For instance, a human being grows from birth to old age, but not from old age to birth. A society grows from agricultural to industrial, but not from industrial to agricultural. Office work goes from typewriters to computers, but not from computers to typewriters. Goods and services go from older markets to newer markets, but not from newer markets to older markets. Examples go on and on.

Not just the one-way movement, entropy also has the water-like ability of spreading, leveling, and equalizing, especially in economic sense. Economic growth, for instance, spreads from more developed areas to less developed ones, raises standards, levels the fields, equalizes markets, and creates opportunities everywhere.

I would like to think of international trade in the "entropy" way, too.

As if with an innate force to flow out and spread out, people from various continents, nations and cultures had always tried since ancient times to reach out to other continents, nations and cultures and to trade. When a country or region was closed to the rest of the world, it was either asked to open or forced to open. As a result, nations have become more and more open, and more and more connected. Once they did, it was hard, if not impossible, to go back to be closed or disconnected again.

In 1947, two years after the WWII, the GATT (General Agreement of Tariffs & Trade) came into being. The purpose of the charter members in establishing such an international trade entity was to create a general, fair and regulated trading structure among nations with different levels of economic and technological development, different products and services, different currencies, different trade practices, and of course, different tariff systems, and to set up through consensus general rules for member countries to follow as well as for the organization to mediate and solve disputes with in the post-war world. In 1995, the GATT became the WTO (World Trade Organization). Its fundamental principle, however, remained the same: non-discrimination among members. So did the key element in its process: consensus.

In a word, the purpose of the WTO, or the GATT before it, seemed to be the achievement of equalization, level

93

field and fair play in international trade so that each member nation could benefit on an equal footing. Although all the effort in international trade as well as in the WTO has been human and economic, I could see the physical law of entropy, especially its force of uniformity, in the process.

The opponents of the WTO may have their legitimate concerns, ranging from the protection of the environment to the protection of labor, from preserving democracy to preserving national sovereignty. But there was one thing they may not have considered, one thing that may have very well been behind all this and beyond the control of all the members or ministers of the WTO: this entropy-like force. It was this force that "pushed" the change of nations from closed to open, from isolated to integrated; it was this force that "pushed" the movement of capital, goods, business, technology and jobs from saturated markets to emerging markets, from high-cost markets to low-cost markets. In a word, all international trade was like water that would fill up low lands and heat that would fill up cold spaces.

That this force seemed so powerful may be because it was also natural. And just like nature, it could be sunny, or rainy.

The movement of jobs, for instance, could be an example.

In 2001, an old sporting goods manufacturer in Washington state announced that it would close its ski production in the area, layoff its employees, and ship the work to China. As a local institution, its closure shocked, agonized and disappointed the community. Many residents, however, understood the position American manufacturing was in. One summed up well, "It kind of hurt our feelings that the work was going someplace else, but, at the same time, we understand the economics: if you can't get the work done cheaper, then you have to do it someplace else."

The story also summed up the whole phenomenon of off-shoring and out-sourcing that American businesses and jobs have experienced in recent decades. Like those sporting goods-manufacturing jobs, textile and garment-making jobs, electronic assembling jobs, hand tool-making jobs, footwear, toy, souvenir and gift-making jobs, and many other household- and light industrial product-making jobs had left the U.S. for East Asia first, and then for China.

It was understandable that with China's WTO accession and the fear of more jobs to lose to lower-paid Chinese workers as well as lower-priced Chinese goods, America's labor unions had worked hard to block it. But blocking China trade was as futile as stopping water from flowing down or heat from spreading around. Just as water would always flow and heat would always spread, jobs and manufacturing would always move as long as there was a cost difference. But the moving would stop when the cost was equalized everywhere in the world. That was not only an issue of cost and profit, or sales and marketing; it was also one of entropy.

The entropy-like development seems to constitute all our life and history. Americans, for instance, crossed the vast land from the "old" New England and to settle in the "new" wilderness on the West Coast; we moved from crowded urban centers to more spacious suburbs; we sell airplanes to countries where they do not make airplanes; we hook up communities to the Internet where people are not yet on-line; we open McDonald's where there are no Big Macs; we open Starbucks where there is no latte; we are still developing new markets for American IT, automobiles, telecommunications, banking, insurance, energy and environmental technologies, etc. when ours are already developed. And we would keep doing so, like water flowing and heat spreading, until people everywhere in the world can enjoy the same products and services. But again, there may be other planets to colonize, to flow and to spread to.

95

Just as we can't make water flow upward or heat spread from cold to warm spaces, we can't expect jobs to move from developing countries to developed ones, or ourselves to move back to the 13 original colonies. Just as we can't stop water from flowing down and heat from filling up cold spaces, we can't prevent business, capital, goods and technology from going to newer markets.

We may slow the process down, make it more fair, but we won't be able stop it. Because the world, with every one of us in it, seems to be moving, relentlessly, towards equalization, equilibrium and uniformity, just like the effect of entropy in thermodynamics.

One big difference may be that while entropy turns order into disorder in thermal energy, the entropy-like force in social and economic sense would turn an un-equal world into an equal one. And there is no turning back.

        🐦   🐦   🐦   🐦   🐦

23. Nuclear Haves vs. Nuclear Have-Nots

Chinese proverb: 只许州官放火，不许百姓点灯
Pronunciation: Zhi Xu Zhou Guan Fang Huo, Bu Xu Bai Xing Dian Deng
Translation: A Magistrate Can Set Fire While Folks Can't Light Lanterns

In Song dynasty China, there was a prefecture magistrate known for his despotic and arbitrary ways. Since *deng* was his given name, he forbade use of any word that had the same sound. A substitute had to be used in place. People who broke the rule were charged as insulting officials, flogged, and even put in jail. Then came the Chinese New Year, along with the traditional lantern festival. The word "lantern" had the same sound as *deng*. In a poster announcing that people could light their lanterns as usual, the magistrate's office used the word "fire" in place of "lantern." Since "light fire" was similar to "set fire," folks were angry and amused at the same time. They jeered, "Your magistrate can set fire, we folks can't light lanterns!" The story became a proverb that would later be used to describe how those with power could do whatever they pleased while putting great restrictions on those without.

I recalled this proverb whenever I heard the nuclear weapons issue in the news.

We all know that these "weapons of mass destruction" could destroy mankind. But they are in the hands of only a few members of this mankind. There are five officially recognized nuclear weapons states, namely the United States, Russia, the United Kingdom, France and China. They seem entitled to the privilege. There are four "unofficially recognized" nuclear weapons states, namely India, Pakistan, Israel and North Korea. They seem less or not entitled to the privilege. Then there was Iraq. The mere suspicion of Iraq having a nuclear weapons program was the main reason for the Bush administration to launch the chaotic and prolonged war against that country. There is also Iran on the radar, since it is believed to have a nuclear weapons program, too. With President Bush's declaration that we could not let Iran have nuclear weapons, another war may be possible. In the meantime, the United States, with the help of China in the six-party talks, has worked hard towards the dismantling of North Korea's nuclear weapons program. So, when a few privileged are allowed to have "weapons of mass destruction" while others are not, doesn't it look like a case where "A magistrate can set fire while folks can't light lanterns?"

We also know that there is a Nuclear Non-Proliferation Treaty (NPT), which was signed by 189 countries, including nuclear as well as non-nuclear states. We have heard a lot about two of the Treaty's main themes, namely non-proliferation and peaceful use of nuclear technology. But there is a third one, disarmament, as stated clearly in its Preamble:

> "Desiring to further the easing of international tension and the strengthening of trust between States in order to facilitate the cessation of the manufacture of nuclear weapons, the liquidation of all their existing stockpiles, and the elimination from national arsenals of nuclear weapons and the means of their delivery pursuant to a Treaty on general and complete disarmament under strict and effective international control ..."

Cessation, liquidation, elimination, and disarmament? So NPT was designed and signed not only to prevent proliferation of nuclear weapons but also to get rid of nuclear weapons? These are topics we have rarely heard discussed or even mentioned by the U.S. government. All its effort seems to have been devoted to the prevention of non-nuclear states from becoming nuclear. Besides, instead of making a serious effort in nuclear weapons disarmament, U.S. government has in fact conducted research and tests during the Bush administration on new tactical nuclear weapons, called bunker-busting or earth-penetrating weapons, spurred by the wars in Afghanistan and Iraq. In 2006, it was reported, President Bush even planned to use those bunker-busters on Iran. So, when a few privileged are allowed to have "weapons of mass destruction," and further develop them, too, while other are not, doesn't it also look like a case where "A magistrate can set fire while folks can't light lanterns?"

The nuclear weapon issue in the world can seem very complicated. It is also very simple. It is not unlike the gun issue in the United States. If gun rights activists could argue that America would be a safer place when more people owned guns, they should also be able to argue that the world be a safer place when more countries had nuclear weapons. If people without guns could feel threatened by those with guns, then countries without nuclear weapons could also feel threatened by those with nuclear weapons. If people without guns would want to own guns to feel safer among those with guns, countries without nuclear weapons would also want to own nuclear weapons to feel safer among those with nuclear weapons.

One good example would be China. During the 1950s and 1960s, China was poor and isolated. Poor because it had just established a new government after decades of war. Isolated because it was a socialist country that Western countries, such as the United States, refused to recognize. Things got worse in the late 1950s when relations between China and the Soviet Union, two otherwise socialist brotherly countries, deteriorated because of ideological disputes. China was thus faced with two hostile powers, the United States and the Soviet Union, both nuclear weapon states. It was under these circumstances that China began developing its nuclear weapons and succeeded in 1964, even though the Chinese people had to live with tightened belts.

But the real reason for China to develop nuclear weapons was not poverty or ideology. It was fear, simple and basic, the fear of nuclear attacks. It was the same fear that prompted North Korea to develop its nuclear weapons. It was the same fear that prompted India and Pakistan to develop their nuclear weapons. It was the same fear that prompted Israel to develop its nuclear weapons. It was the same fear that prompted Russia, even Britain and France, to develop their nuclear weapons, after, of course, the United States had developed its first.

As long as there are nuclear weapons in the world, so it seems, there will be fear, legitimate fear, therefore legitimate reason, for a non-nuclear country to want to become a nuclear one. Yet, when one country, the United States, had been free to develop nuclear weapons for its own security, four other countries then developed nuclear weapons out of fear of nuclear attacks, while the rest of the world has been forbidden to develop nuclear weapons out of the same fear, doesn't it look again like a case where "A magistrate can set fire while folks can't light lanterns?"

It seems pretty clear that to truly prevent non-nuclear countries from developing nuclear weapons, their fear of nuclear attacks has to be removed. That means all countries should work together on all aspects of the NPT treaty, especially towards the common goal of a general and complete disarmament of nuclear weapons in the world.

Or a "world without nuclear weapons," as called for in early 2007 and again in early 2008 by four prominent security experts of the nation: George P. Shultz, William Perry, Henry Kissinger and Sam Nunn. They pointed out that the U.S., along with Russia, had to demonstrate leadership in creating that world. They also pointed out Iran and many other non-nuclear countries had long complained about the "double standard" of nuclear powers in possessing atomic weapons while demanding that others refrain from having them.

Let's hope that the United States, with the largest nuclear arsenal of all, will take the lead in this effort. Otherwise, it would still look like a case where "A magistrate can set fire while folks can't light lanterns."

Part 3. American Politics

24. Everyone a Saint Before Hart?

Chinese saying: 假正经
Pronunciation: Jia Zheng Jing
Translation: Pretending to Be a Saint

While in the graduate program, I followed the campaigns for the 1988 presidential election. It was the first American political drama I ever watched up close. I didn't know what to expect. Leading the Democratic pack was Gary Hart, a former U.S. Senator from Colorado.

About a month into his campaign in the spring of 1987, the Donna Rice story broke. The photo of Hart with Rice sitting in his lap splashed across newspapers and television screens. In a week, Hart withdrew his otherwise promising race. It was an astonishing as well as puzzling turn of event to me.

Before coming to America, I had gotten pretty good a measure of exposure to the country. I had read American history, read about the anti-war movement of the 1960s, along with the hippies, had access to American magazines and newspapers, used American English textbooks, listened to Voice of America, followed the normalization of China-U.S. relations, and even held a job working for visiting American delegations. In addition, I had also watched a number of American television shows on Hong Kong television broadcast in southern China, especially *Dallas*, the hit American television soap opera of the 1980s. The show's popularity and long running seemed to say that Americans had a lot in common with or aspired to the way of life, including love and marriage, of the Ewings. It added to my impression that American mores regarding sex were quite relaxed.

The real life next to me also enhanced that impression. My landlord, for instance, a widower, had a steady girl friend in a married woman. Not only did they get together frequently in his place, he also had porn video on all the time. I often had to resort to plugging my ears because the noise never failed to come through the wood panel wall separating my studio apartment and his living room.

Therefore in my mind, a fling or an affair shouldn't have been too much out of the ordinary in the United States. That's why it surprised me to see how media hunted Hart down, staked out his residence, exposed his Monkey Business the yacht, and asked him embarrassing questions such as "Do you think adultery is immoral?" "Have you ever committed adultery?"

Why the sudden innocence among the American public regarding the Hart-Rice story, I wondered, in a land where "free love" had been celebrated by a generation and adultery glorified in TV shows? Why the relentless scrutiny of Hart's personal life when his wife Lee herself had already come out and stood by her husband? The Chinese saying in the title came to my mind, in the form of a question: Was this not a case of "Pretending to be a saint," in other words, hypocrisy?

I expressed my bewilderment to my fellow graduate students and professors at lunch breaks. Wasn't everybody doing it? What's the big deal? I asked. No, everybody was not doing it, of course not, they said. They told me how magazine stories or soap operas could be far from the reality of American society and also how a candidate for a high public office should have been held up to a higher standard, etc. They were even amused that I had been watching *Dallas*. Upon catching me once following an episode of *Dallas* in the computer room, the director of the program quipped, "Hey, we didn't bring you here to watch *Dallas!*"

They may have been right, with some of them being family men with children, etc. In December that year, the result of the New Hampshire primary proved them to be. Gary Hart, after re-entering the race, received only 4% of the vote.

Not too long after that, after moving from Atlanta to Seattle, a brief experience with another family man demonstrated to me again how upright, or uptight, a married American man could be.

I had become friends with a married couple with children, a typical American family in a typical American suburb. I visited them in their house a number of times, but not alone. One day, however, I needed to deliver a computer disk to the husband who was alone at home, working on his own business. When I arrived, he had stepped out the house to greet me and didn't invite me in. We talked for a while on the porch before we said good-bye. I felt a little odd, but realized afterwards: my friend must have tried to avoid the potential appearance of impropriety in meeting me alone in their house, especially in the eyes of his cul-de-sac neighbors. How discreet! I never knew anybody in China that had done that.

In later years, I saw more and more examples how ordinary Americans cherished and celebrated their marriage and family, how both liberals and conservatives alike constantly emphasized family values, how politicians took special pride in presenting their spouses and/or families in front of voters, etc. It was quite an eye-opener for me, in two ways: One, it was very different from my previous impression of America based on the sexual revolution and free love of the 1960s or *Dallas* of the 1980s. Two, it was also very different from China where family and marriage had always been valued but seldom talked about and almost never shown off.

So I was wrong about American people's rejection of Gary Hart as a presidential candidate over his immoral behavior in the late 1980s. They weren't "Pretending to be a saint." They were for real.

That was at least the lesson then.

25. It Varies with Clinton?

Chinese proverb: 因人而异
Pronunciation: Yin Ren Er Yi
Translation: It Varies with Each Individual

It was puzzling to me in 1987 to see Gary Hart shot down at the height of his presidential race because of his liaison with Donna Rice. I had thought then that such liaisons should have been nothing to Americans since extra-marital affairs were common in the American society.

A decade later, in 1998, I was puzzled again, more so this time: The American public made a U turn in their position regarding extra-marital affairs of their political leaders, specifically President Clinton this time.

With a string of earlier affairs and ultimately the scandal with Monica Lewinsky on the part of President Clinton, an overwhelming majority of American voters consistently, or inconsistently, gave him high approval ratings and chose to ignore his adulterous behavior in the White House.

With what Bill Clinton did in the Oval Office many times more serious than what Gary Hart had done on his campaign trail, I expected the American public to feel much more disappointed if not disgusted with Clinton than they had felt about Hart. Why the difference in their attitude towards the two affairs which were basically the same in nature? Was it as the Chinese proverb in the title said, "It varies with each individual" when it came to their beliefs or principles?

Compared with their view in 1987, was the new attitude in 1998 a sign of American voters' maturity or regression, pragmatism or cynicism, selfishness or generosity, or simply materialism, meaning as long as the economy was good, who

108

cared if the prestige of the White House and American family values were down the tubes? It was hard to tell. To me, one thing for sure was that Americans had changed in the decade in between their moral standard for politicians in high office. That was regretful, for I had begun to view Americans in a new light of awe with their rejection of Gary Hart. Now 10 years later, my old view was beckoning again.

There came later, however, a subtle change in the public opinion polls that year. A typical one showed that while a majority of Americans still gave high marks to Clinton's job performance, they also expressed doubt that President Clinton still shared their values. With that, the American public seemed to have decided to make a clear separation of their President's public life and private life, as if the two had no effect on or no relation whatsoever with each other.

So a politician's private life, especially his extra-marital affairs, could be separated from his public life after all? That's what I had thought in 1987 about Gary Hart in the first place, but the American public had thought otherwise.

And a politician should be judged only by his job performance even if he engaged in immoral behavior, outrageously immoral behavior for that matter, in his private life? That's what I had thought in 1987 about Gary Hart, but the American public had thought otherwise.

Which way was it then? Should we or should we not separate our political leaders' private life from their public one? Should we or should we not judge our politicians by their job performance only?

Surprisingly, these questions were not new, nor were they American only. They were asked not just about American presidents; they had also been asked about Chinese emperors.

The Tang dynasty, for instance, was the peak of the Chinese civilization. It was often referred to as the "Prosperous

Tang." Traders and scholars from various regions and countries in the world traveled to and lived in its capital Chang'an, today's Xi'an. Literature, arts and crafts also reached their height under Tang. Yet at the same time, Tang emperors were also among the most corrupt in China's history. Emperor Li Longji, for example, who had reined from 712 to 756, was one example. Anyone who has been a tourist to Xi'an probably also visited the site of the Huaqing Hot Spring palace Emperor Li had built for his royal concubine Yang Guifei, or Imperial Concubine Yang. He indulged himself so much with Yang and became so negligent of his official duties during the later years of his throne that he suffered a powerful rebellion by one of his generals and had to witness the death by hanging of Yang. Yet, during the early years of his reign, Emperor Li had also carried out various government reforms and brought major economic development in the country. Because of his achievement, Chinese historians credited him as "having opened a new era" for China.

So how should Emperor Li be judged? A good emperor or bad emperor? A good emperor who led a corrupt life or a bad emperor who did a good job?

I guess, as the Chinese proverb "It varies with each individual" suggested, each individual was different, so was each individual case. That at least was the impression I got from the American public's respective, and opposite, views towards Gary Hart and Bill Clinton in a span of a decade. They seemed to say: Well, there is no standard. It all depends.

I should continue to stay tuned.

᠊ᡦ   ᡦ   ᡦ   ᡦ   ᡦ

26. First Lady and First Wife

Chinese saying: 三从四德
Pronunciation: San Cong Si De
Translation: The Three Obediences and Four Virtues

With the help of the civil rights movement and legislation such as affirmative action, women's movement narrowed the gap between American men and women tremendously, in employment, education, family life, etc. As a woman, Hillary Clinton's professional achievement was an example of women's achievement as a whole. As the First Lady, the first professional First Lady for that matter, she also became as a symbol of all American women as well as women's lib.

It was against this background that her reaction as the First Lady, or lack of, in 1998, towards President Clinton's scandal with Monica Lewinsky seemed all the more incomprehensible. It raised great doubt in my mind as to what women's movement had really achieved, in domestic front in this case, as in the First Family. Virginia Slims commercial used to say: "You've come a long way, baby." Did we really?

Patricia Ireland, then president of National Organization for Women (NOW), described Hillary's supportiveness to her husband as showing "dignity." Was it dignity? In the same period, the First Lady received very high approval ratings, surprisingly from more women than men, for her commitment to her marriage that, to everyone else with a common sense, looked more like Swiss cheese. Why the commitment?

For thousands of years, women from East to West were oppressed in various ways and treated as property, slaves, sex objects, or trophy. One cruel practice against women was polygamy, or polygyny, where a rich man had, or owned, a

111

number of wives, as in the traditional Chinese society, for instance.

Anyone who watched the Chinese movie *Raising the Red Lantern* probably got an idea about this kind of marriage. As in the movie, the wives in such an arrangement suffered not only the suffocating dead-end marriage to the same man, rarely with love, but also the unavoidable strife among themselves.

However, this kind of marriage was hardest on the first wife, the official wife. Imagine you were chosen by a man to be his first wife because of your comparable family status as well as political, financial, social and other usefulness such an alliance would bring him. Then your husband would keep adding newer and younger wives for beauty, lust, procreation, or love. You may have certain social status outwardly, but inside, your heart was bleeding. But no matter how miserable you were, you put on your best smile every day and carried on with family and social obligations as the first wife. You cried your lonely nights, swallowed your tears, and suffered without words. That was because you knew what was required of a good woman by the "Three Obediences and Four Virtues," the ancient commandments for Chinese women from as early as the Han dynasty, 200 BC-200 AD.

The Three Obediences were as follows: a woman should obey her father before marriage, obey her husband after marriage, and obey her son after the death of her husband. The Four Virtues were morality, proper speech, modest manner, and diligent work.

Under those commandments, a woman in an unhappy polygamous or arranged marriage would willingly live on unhappily for the happiness and honor of her husband and his family, but never hers. That was considered dignity.

How ironic that the "dignity" of the First Lady of the United States, the most advanced and modern society in the world, in the face of the president's notorious affair, not to say a string of other illicit relationships on the part of the president throughout their marriage, looked so similar to the dignity of those miserable women in traditional marriages of an earlier era! Was it dignity or indignity? It may have been dignity in the pre-women's lib age, but on the eve of the 21st century?

The whole point of women's movement was to get rid of all the indignity, inequality, injustice and inhumanness against women as in the traditional societies. But if women, such as Hillary Clinton in this case, did not mind putting up with the indignity in their relationship with men and accepting it as necessary for the sake of marriage or status, etc., why did we need a women's lib?

There may have been degrees of difference being a first wife in a polygamous marriage sharing a husband with his multiple wives vs. being a wife in a regular marriage sharing a husband with multiple third women. There may have also been degrees of difference being forced to obey one's husband for family honor vs. submitting willingly to one's husband for political reasons. But shutting one's eyes to the problem, swallowing one's tears of anguish, accepting the outrageous as necessary, and even defending the wrongdoing of one's husband, as the First Lady did, was the same strategy a first wife in an unhappy polygamous or arranged marriage in a traditional society had to adopt.

It was a pity that women's organizations such as NOW believed that Hillary Clinton was women's role model when she defended President Clinton over his scandal. But her reaction was really a 1990s reflection at the highest level of thousands of years of oppression against women who had to sacrifice their own happiness for the sake of their men, plus some power and influence in her case.

The bigger pity was that Hillary Clinton never realized that she shared the same "dignity" of a miserable first wife in a polygamous marriage under the Three Obediences and

113

Four Virtues commandments. That was as disappointing, if not more, as having the president of the United States caught with his pants down in the Oval Office.

  🐦   🐦   🐦   🐦   🐦

27. Confucius' Golden Mean and the Middle Way Politics

Chinese proverb: 中庸之道
Pronunciation: Zhong Yong Zhi Dao
Translation: The Doctrine of the Mean

One thing in American politics that has interested me was what was in between the two main parties, or the converging zone of the two, mentioned as the moderate, the middle, the centrist, the independents, the purple, etc.

The word centrist was heard a lot after the 2006 midterm election, as the election sent many centrists to state and federal legislatures. The best example of centrist politics was perhaps the governor of California Arnold Schwarzenegger, who had run as a Republican, worked well with a Democratic-dominated state legislature, easily won a second term, and called for a new and creative center in post-partisanship.

Last time centrist politics was in fad in force was the 1990s, in the United States as well as in other major western democracies. There was Bill Clinton, of course, president of the U.S., representing the New Democrats. There was Tony Blair, Prime Minister of Britain and an architect of the New Labour. There was Gerhard Shroeder, chancellor of Germany, a social democrat and a moderate ex-Marxist. Together, their middle of the way politics was dubbed the Third Way.

Best to explain the Third Way was perhaps Anthony Giddens, British sociologist and author of *The Third Way*. He said, "With the rapid shrinking of the working class and the disappearance of the bipolar world, the salience of class politics, as well as the traditional divisions of left and right, has diminished."

Best to represent the Third Way was perhaps Bill Clinton. On the one hand, Clinton was a typical Democrat president. He created the ambiguous "Don't ask, don't tell" gay policy for the military. He put First Lady Hillary Clinton in charge of a national health care plan. He favored micromanaging programs for schools, such as hiring more teachers, making classes smaller, etc. He appointed the first woman secretary of state as well as minority members in his cabinet to make it look more like America. He never wavered in his support for affirmative action. He was firm on crimes, tobacco and gun control, too. On the other hand, he also acted like a Republican president and even declared that the era of big government was over. He carried out welfare reforms in cooperation with a Republican Congress. He balanced the budget on his watch. He advocated family values with family-friendly bills. He expanded and strengthened NATO, especially with the war in Yugoslavia. He supported international trade. He even outdid President Nixon in carrying out a policy of all-round engagement and strategic partnership with China.

Be it called centrist or the Third Way or other names in modern politics, the middle way politics reminded me of the ancient doctrine of the mean of Kong Zi, or Confucius, the Chinese philosopher who lived from 551-479 BC.

As one of the leading theories of the Confucian school of thought, the doctrine of the mean suggested that all things should be handled in an even-handed, impartial and unbiased way, without tilting to one side or leaning to the other, without being either deficient or excessive. The middle position, as explained in the theory, was the highest standard of moral behavior.

Regrettably, Confucius was condemned in China during the Cultural Revolution, which was the most excessive of revolutions. The Confucian school of thought was criticized as one that served the interests of the exploiting class. The doctrine of the mean and teachings of moderation were considered un-revolutionary, if not counter-revolutionary. And the studies of Confucius were banned.

The reforms over the recent decades, however, have revived Confucius studies as well as China's economy. Not only has Confucius become popular again, Confucian teachings have also been incorporated into the governing theories of the Chinese government. The new policy under President Hu Jintao of building a harmonious society in China may be the best example, as harmony was one of the trademark Confucian teachings.

The centrist theory was, of course, not just Confucian. About a hundred some years after Confucius, Aristotle, the Greek philosopher, also established a similar set of thoughts crystallized in the Greek word "mesotes," meaning the middle of two extremes. He believed that all human behavior fell into three ways: excessive, deficient and medium. Only the medium, he pointed out, represented excellence of virtue.

Besides Chinese and Greek philosophy, the theory of the happy medium was also American, found in American folklore of all places. As told in *Goldilocks and the Three Bears*, the children's story, wherein the porridge had to be just right, not too hot and not too cold, the theory was dubbed, happily, the Goldilocks Theory.

But no matter it was Confucius' golden mean, or Aristotle's mesotes, or Goldilocks' porridge, they all seemed to teach us the same lesson of human wisdom: moderation.

Moderation, such as avoiding extremes and incorporating differences from both left and right, could be good politics, as Bill Clinton demonstrated in the 1990s. Moderation, such as not too liberal, not too conservative, has also been the position of majority of American voters who are mostly in the middle.

After all, middle way just seems so sensible, feasible and practical a way for politics as well as for life in general. Let's stay in the middle.

❧ ❧ ❧ ❧ ❧

28. Left and Right in American and Chinese Politics

Chinese saying: 形左实右, 形右实左
Pronunciation: Xing Zuo Shi You, Xing You Shi Zuo
Translation: Left in Form but Right in Essence
and Right in Form but Left in Essence

Left and right were the most basic directions we learned from the earliest days of our lives. Yet left and right could also be the most sophisticated terms and concepts in modern politics—American politics in particular, especially to a relatively new voter like me.

There were, first of all, the two main parties, the Republican Party and the Democratic Party, and the two main terms used to describe them, liberal and conservative. These terms were then used in crisscross fashion with numerous combinations. On the Democratic side, for instance, there were Conservative Democrats, Liberal Democrats, Libertarian Democrats, New Democrats, Centrists, Progressive Democrats, etc., and of course, Reagan Democrats. On the Republican side, there were Religious Right, Neoconservatives, Social Conservatives, Fiscal Conservatives, Paleoconservatives, Libertarians, Moderates, Liberals, and Log Cabin Republicans, etc., and not to forget President Bush's "compassionate conservatism."

It seemed that one could be right and left or left and right at the same time. Or as the Chinese saying suggests, one could be "Left in form but right in essence, or right in form but left in essence." It was truly a maze, a maze of left and right!

But before this American maze, I had experienced the Chinese one.

119

For many years, life in China was an endless series of political movements led by the Chinese Communist Party. Those political movements, in turn, had their corresponding inner party factional struggles. Although the party itself was on the very left of the political spectrum, it had its own left, right, ultra-left and ultra-right factions within its own ranks. Although it consistently attacked the right, it also attacked those who were "Left in form but right in essence," meaning those who may have appeared to be on the left but in nature were really on the right. Lin Biao, the one time Defense Minister and Vice Chairman of the Central Military Commission, was a good example. As Mao's handpicked successor, Lin had been the one who created the Little Red Book of Mao quotations and extolled Mao to the skies. In appearance, he was the most leftward person in China and the biggest Maoist. Yet, Lin was also the one who later plotted a coup d'etat against Mao. After that failed, Lin fled in a frenzy to the Soviet Union, the "social-imperialist" power and the arch enemy of China's in those years, an extremely "right" move to take, but died in a plane crash before reaching there.

Besides maze, left and right could also be in a circle. In the late 1980s, I met an economics professor, Dr. Zhang, from Hong Kong, at a seminar in China. Dr. Zhang had been a professor in the U.S. and known the late Milton Friedman and other economists. In our conversation, Zhang told me a theory of his, a "weird circle," as he called it, of politics. If you lined up all the political positions from left to right along a circle, he explained to me, extreme left would meet extreme right. That was so clever, I thought.

Years later, when I began to try to understand American politics, I remembered Dr. Zhang's circle. Now I thought it was brilliant, brilliant especially on how extreme right would meet extreme left along the circle. Or better, the two did not only meet along an imaginary circle, they had also met in person!

Anyone who read about China's Cultural Revolution had an idea how left China had been. Domestically, there was total repudiation of all that was not socialist, total loyalty to Mao and Mao's teachings, total obedience to the communist party, total faith in the cause of communism, and total command of proletarian politics in everything from economy to education. Internationally, there was alliance with all socialist countries and the Third World against Western capitalist powers, and brotherhood with communist parties around the world in the common struggle to overthrow all reactionary governments.

Yet, it was at the height of that ultra-left revolution that, Mao Zedong, the ultimate leader of Chinese communists, reached out and shook hands with Richard Nixon, the one-time top red-baiter and highest representative of the very right of the "imperialist" America. What was more, they hit it off famously. That episode was perhaps the most fascinating example in world politics of the extreme left meeting the extreme right!

But Dr. Zhang's "weird circle" did not work only in "extreme" cases; it worked in "regular" politics, too, where the very left met the very right.

Richard Gephardt and Patrick Buchanan were a good example. The one on the left was a former House Minority Leader, senior liberal Democrat and two-time Democratic Party presidential candidate. The one on the right was a leading conservative writer and two-time Republican Party presidential candidate and one time Reform Party presidential candidate. Yet they shared the exact same view on trade with China. Gephardt voted no on Permanent Normal Trade Relations with China in 2000. Buchanan called the U.S.-China bilateral agreement on China's accession to the World Trade Organization a complete sellout by the Clinton administration.

121

In more recent years, a similar drama played out between another pair of left and right politicians: Charles Schumer and Lindsey Graham. The one on the left was senior Democratic U.S. Senator from New York and Vice Chairman of the Senate Democratic Caucus. The one on the right was senior Republican U.S. Senator from South Carolina and member of the Senate Arms Services and Judiciary Committees. Yet the two were happy co-sponsors of a bill that advocated imposing a 27.5 percent tariff on all Chinese goods entering the United States as retaliation to what they believed to be the reason of the huge U.S. trade deficit with China: the undervalued Chinese currency *yuan*.

Using the Chinese saying "Left in form but right in essence and right in form but left in essence," who among Gephardt, Buchanan, Schumer and Graham was truly left or truly right, or left or right only in form but not in essence?

The meeting of the very left and the very right did not only happen across the aisle of the U.S. Congress, it also took place across the Pacific between Chinese and American politicians, especially on U.S.-China relations. On the very right, for instance, were American conservative hawks who saw China as a Cold-War and Soviet-Union-type enemy and believed that China had always wanted to become another superpower to compete with the United States in the world, in Asia in particular. On the very left were the conservative hardliners in the Chinese communist leadership who never trusted the United States and believed that United States had always wanted to be the sole superpower, dominate the world, contain China, and impose American views and system on China and the rest of the world. So the Chinese conservatives from the very left and the American conservatives from the very right in fact mirrored, if not met, each other in their views!

The left and the right do not just "mirror" each other; they also "mix" with each other, especially in terms of political systems. China, for instance, is still officially a socialist country. Yet it practices capitalism in its economy. Most Western democracies are capitalist countries, yet some have welfare systems that are socialist to various degrees. Where would they be placed on Dr. Zhang's "weird circle"?

With rapid changes and increasing exchanges in the world economically, technologically and ideologically, the maze of politics would surely become more and more confusing. But it seems safe to say that in the world of politics, left or right, democratic or republican, socialist or capitalist, etc. may not be exactly or totally what they "appear" to be. In "essence," there is right in left, left in right, democratic in republican, republican in democratic, capitalist in socialist, and socialist in capitalist. It is all a-maze-ing.

29. American Politicians' Self-Selling

Chinese proverb: 毛遂自荐
Pronunciation: Mao Sui Zi Jian
Translation: Mao Sui Who Recommends Himself

The United States and China have many differences between them. One can get a serious culture shock going from one country to the other. I have been asked about my culture shock in the U.S. Of a number of things that could be considered a shock, the most "shocking" for me, however, was political "culture."

I am not talking about the whole culture of politics, only one aspect of it: the self-selling of the politicians.

I remember observing my first American presidential campaigns in the late 1980s. It was really an eye-opening experience. Each candidate, Democratic or Republican, promoted or bragged about himself, including his experience, ideas, achievement, policies, family, upbringing, etc. Each believed himself to be the best for the job. Each stated, "When I am president of the United States of America, I will do this and that..." They acted in such an unabashed way that it could be seen as shameless in Chinese culture, at least for someone fresh from China.

Since then, I have followed a number of election seasons in the United States, and even voted in a few. But I still haven't got used to the selling part of the elections, especially the "blowing one's own trumpet" part.

One reason was, of course, the different political system I used to know and live under in China where elections were just not a big part of life. But there was another reason, a stronger and cultural one. Let me start with the Chinese

124

proverb story: *Mao Sui zi jian*, or Mao Sui who recommends himself.

Mao Sui lived in the years of China's Warring States period between 400 and 200 BC. The State of Zhao was being attacked by the State of Qin. The King of Zhao decided to send a team of 20 civil and military officials to the State of Chu with a proposal for an alliance against Qin. He had 19 officials. Mao Sui, a consultant for Zhao, stepped up and recommended his own service. He was accepted. Negotiations with Chu dragged on for hours without progress. Mao Sui stepped up again, a sword in hand, and eloquently laid out all the benefits from such an alliance as well as disadvantages without it. He succeeded in persuading the king of Chu to form the alliance with Zhao. A ceremony was held with animal blood applied to participants' faces. Mao Sui became a hero. His story became a proverb used to describe somebody who would recommend himself and take on a difficult task.

Mao Sui's story was well known in China and the proverb was used frequently in daily life. But in the Chinese understanding of the proverb, what any one should recommend oneself for, like Mao Sui did, was never something associated with high office, power, or prestige. On the contrary, it was often something unpleasant, uncomfortable, or even dangerous.

For instance, a student might recommend himself and stay behind after school to help the teacher with papers; a soldier in a battle might recommend himself and risk his life to provide cover for his comrades; a worker might recommend himself and do extra work after hours when others were unavailable; a college graduate might recommend himself and take a job in a remote area rather than stay behind in a big city for a more comfortable life, etc.

As for high office or leadership positions, the Chinese thinking was very different. In the Chinese mind, no one should think or say that he or she was better, not to say best,

125

in anything. People were supposed to do their best and let others judge if they were good or not. Modesty was very important in Chinese culture. People promoting or bragging about themselves were frowned upon. There was a proverb just for that kind of people and behavior, with a degree of contempt, too: Lady Wang who boasts about the watermelons she sells. Even when a person were recommended by others for a position, he or she would always, as expected to, state that he or she was not good enough for it and that there were others who were better or more suitable.

In America, of course, it was 180-degree different. Everybody, every politician at least, was a boastful Lady Wang.

But my "shock" at the political self-selling has been wearing off a bit. I came to see that America's political "culture" of selling is the counterpart of its economic "culture" of selling. In a market economy, people had to sell their products, services or skills. In a "market politics," politicians had to sell their ideas, experience and policies.

Talk about economic "culture." With several decades of reforms, China's economy is more and more market-oriented, with more than half now in private hands. Selling has become as important a part of life in China as in America. A question arises: Would the new economic "culture" of selling help develop a new political "culture" of selling in China?

In fact, elections have been held at village, township and county levels in China since the late 1970s. Elections at municipal and provincial levels have also been discussed for the future. But I am not sure if the Chinese, politicians and voters, would be comfortable with political self-selling one day.

If they will, I would have a culture shock the other way. But I would also wonder what it would sound like if a future Chinese presidential candidate says to the crowd at a campaign rally, in Chinese, of course, "When I am president of China, I will..."

30. Taking Others' Money in American Politics

Chinese saying: 吃人家的嘴软，拿人家的手短
Pronunciation: Chi Ren Jia De Zui Ruan, Na Ren Jia De Shou Duan
Translation: Eating Others' Makes One's Mouth Soft, Taking Others' Makes One's Hands Short

The Chinese saying above says that if you eat food other people give you, you will have soft words to say about them; if you take things other people give you, you will not have long hands to meddle in their affairs. More broadly, it refers to the way people behave after receiving favors, material or non-material. They tend to become very friendly, accommodating, or flattering towards their benefactors, and always ready to repay the favors.

Once upon a time, people in "socialist" China used to criticize everything about "capitalist" America. They dismissed the democratic system in the U.S. as a pretense because they believed that the two political parties had been both controlled by interest groups and big money. I was influenced by that view, too. But there was no way of knowing how much of the "control" was true and how much of it was exaggerated. It was not an issue that really concerned me anyway, not even for a number of years later on living in the United States, until 1999, the year I became a citizen.

In the spring of that year, Bill Moyers, the renowned broadcast journalist and commentator, had a special PBS show on money and politics. "Both parties are controlled, owned and operated by subsidiaries of big money," he said, "even though the money comes from different pockets." He continued, "Republicans take it from gambling interests and Democrats from Hollywood. The Democrats take it from

127

China, the Republicans from Taiwan. Both take it from Israel and politics has become an arms race for money." After giving examples of cases in which money from interest groups and rich industries had overwhelmed political debate and changed or twisted the outcome, Moyers concluded that in American politics, the debate was no longer between left and right but between corporations and the unincorporated. He really got my attention: So the old impression back in China had not been too far-fetched after all.

Oh, money, money. Money was such a fascinating phenomenon. Numerous sayings were created for it, from East to West: "Money makes the mare go," "Money makes the world go round," "Money is the root of all evil," "Money will move the gods," etc. Wondering which saying would describe the money in American politics, I remembered the Chinese saying in the title: "Eating others' makes one's mouth soft. Taking others' makes one's hands short." What about taking others' money?

In the years since the Moyers program, there has been the passing in 2002 of the McCain-Feingold Bill, or the Bipartisan Campaign Reform Act, which banned "soft money" donations to the national Republican and Democratic parties. As a relatively new voter, I admit that I did not fully understand the rules of political campaign financing. But if the bill had meant to limit money in politics or even remove some money from politics, it didn't seem to have worked much. The money raised and spent by political candidates skyrocketed instead of going in the other direction.

In a 2006 speech, Moyers pointed out that in 1996, $1.6 billion had been spent on the congressional and presidential elections; in 2004, he said, that total had more than doubled to $3.9 billion. According to opensecrets.org, in 2000, President Bush spent over $185 million in his campaign, while Al Gore spent over $120 million. In 2004, President Bush raised over $367 million for his re-election, while John Kerry did over $328 million for his bid, making that year's presidential election the most expensive in history. As for the 2008 presidential election, according to *The Washington Post*, Michael E. Toner, chairman of the Federal Election Commission, advised that the entry fee for serious potential presidential candidates for the contests was a neat $100 million.

A natural question to follow was: from whom did the candidates raise all those millions of dollars? Again according to Moyers, in 2004, all that money came from just less than one half of one percent of all Americans, i.e., those who gave $200 and more. If one counts only those who wrote a check of $1,000 and more, the percentage would go down to less than one-tenth of one percent. So, with such a small percentage of Americans directly contributing to the political campaigns, did we still have a representative democracy? Kevin Phillips, a political strategist and scholar on American political and economic history of wealth, didn't think so. He called this fusion of money and government plutocracy.

What I was most interested in, however, was the next aspect of the issue. Since eating others makes one's mouth soft and taking others' makes one's hands short, what would taking others' money make one do?

Back in the 1990s, as we all remember, President Clinton famously repaid the favors to his supporters by selling White House access or privilege, from coffees to photos, from dinners to private movies, from Lincoln bedroom "Bed and Breakfast" to high-level security clearance, etc. He literally turned the people's house into a high-ticket political commodity.

In the era of President Bush, money seems to have been linked more to influence on policies. That was clear from many of the internal memos of the Republican National Committee from 1999 to 2000 submitted to the Supreme Court as evidence. A typical exchange was one memo, for instance, to the then Chairman James Nicholson, concerning a Republican supporter and an oil business owner. It mentioned how many thousands of dollars this gentleman had given the RNC and then discussed how the gentleman was concerned about an estate tax bill, etc.

Between the Democratic Party and the Republican Party, however, there has been a shared practice of awarding presidential appointees to wealthy contributors. For instance, on the Democratic side, John Huang, who had raised 4-5 million dollars for the Democratic Party, was awarded by President Clinton the position of deputy assistant secretary for international economic affairs at the Commerce Department. One the Republican side, according to opensecrets.org, Ronald P. Spogli, a classmate of President Bush's as well as an investment banker who had given the president's party $802,807 in contributions, was repaid the ambassadorship to Italy in 2005. A study released by the Princeton Survey Research in 2001 had this conclusion:

> "It appears that both in the Clinton and Bush administrations money has played a role in appointments, that contributors make up a big share of the pool of potential appointees and, if you don't give, you are less likely to get considered for an appointment...The presidential appointment system is in danger of becoming a kind of spoils system for wealthy contributors."

I guess I could now add a third part to the Chinese saying: Taking others' money makes one kowtow.

With political campaigns, especially presidential campaigns, stretching longer and longer, with more and more dollars needed to run them, kowtowing may not even be the worst part. In an interview on PBS in 2002 over campaign finance, Sen. John McCain quoted Sen. Zell Miller of Georgia: "After a period of fund raising, I felt like a prostitute after a busy day."

Tragic or comic, those words offered a piercing description of how money played a role in American politics and how far politicians would go after it.

The welcome news is that things have already started to change. With "Change we can believe in" as the theme of his presidential campaign, Barack Obama is also changing the way money is raised. Of his 3 million plus donors, half of them contributed $200 or less, with an average donation of less than $100. I am looking forward to understanding money in American politics in a new way.

31. Yesterday's Vietnam and Today's Iraq

Chinese proverb: 早知今日，何必当初
Pronunciation: Zao Zhi Jin Ri, He Bi Dang Chu
Translation: Knowing Today, Wondering Why Yesterday

When I worked as an intern in Washington, D.C. one summer in the late 1980s, I had the fortune of staying with a family in their townhouse near L'Enfant Plaza, a few minutes' walk from the National Mall. One of the first things they told me about the nation's capital was the Vietnam Veterans Memorial and its design by a young Chinese-American woman. So the memorial wall was one of the first places I went to see.

It was a mixed feeling touring the long and inscribed marble wall.

The first thing it reminded me of was the "Forest of Tablets" in my hometown, Xi'an, one of China's ancient capitals: the large collection of stone slabs of various shapes and sizes with elaborate inscriptions passed down over hundreds of years. One could see where the young architect, Maya Lin, got her inspiration. She reportedly was the niece of the first female architect in China.

But more poignantly, it reminded me of the old newspaper stories I had seen in China many years before, stories on how American helicopters frequently got shot down in Vietnam and how Americans were in a sorry plight there. I remembered a cartoon that depicted a John F. Kennedy diving into the ground like a downed helicopter with his nose first. His name was turned into three Chinese characters: bite mud ground, pronounced *ken ni di*, pretty close to its English sounds.

There were, of course, no diplomatic relations between the United States and China when the Vietnam War was going on. To the U.S., China was Red China. To China, the U.S. was the Imperialist U.S. No matter how successive American governments had justified the Vietnam War or the death of over 58,000 American soldiers, whose names were engraved on the wall, as well as that of millions of Vietnamese, the Chinese saw it as an imperialist war, an unjust war. It was also a potentially anti-China war, for it had pushed the American defense line to China's border. The Chinese gave their support to the North Vietnamese, their comrades, who eventually won.

When I stood by the memorial wall that summer, it was almost a decade into normalized relations between the U.S. and China. At the same time, the U.S. and Vietnam were conducting joint investigations on MIAs of the Vietnam War. A roadmap was also in the works on the part of the U.S. government for the normalization of relations with Vietnam. Reflecting on the dramatic turnabout in U.S.-China relations, my thoughts on the Vietnam War were summed up by the Chinese proverb in the title, *"Zao zhi jin ri, he bi dang chu"* or "Knowing today, wondering why yesterday." I wondered if Americans were looking back and wondering, too, about the why of the Vietnam War.

But that of course was a historical issue for the United States as a nation to deal with, not one for me, a student from China, to lose sleep over. I didn't give much thought to Vietnam again until years later, in 2003, when America's war drums were beating hard again, this time, against Iraq. By then, I was an American citizen and anti-Iraq war.

I had the same access as that of most Americans to news and information regarding Iraq, yet I saw no evidence of an imminent threat, no link between Iraq and 9/11, and no nuclear weapons possibly hidden in that country. All I saw was an American president and his administration trumpeting, or "elevating," the threat, as former Secretary of Defense Donald Rumsfeld did, for an unnecessary war.

Interestingly, this time, it was Sen. Edward Kennedy, the younger brother of President Kennedy who first sent American troops to Vietnam, that took the lead in opposing the new war and called Iraq "George Bush's Vietnam." I didn't know if Sen. Kennedy had gone through a process of "Knowing today, wondering why yesterday" about the Vietnam War. His comparison of the Iraq War with the Vietnam War, to me, was a watershed in America's understanding and assessment of its war in the jungle yesterday vs. its war in the desert today. It certainly brought back memories of my tour to the Vietnam Veterans Memorial.

Half of Americans, however, did not think as Sen. Kennedy, or I, did, including a good friend of mine, good until we differed on the Iraq War. A Woodstock-hippie-Democrat-turned-Vietnam veteran and Reagan loyalist, my friend whole-heartedly embraced Bush's policy of unilateral and preemptive wars. He sincerely believed that the Iraqis had buried their nuclear weapons in the sand. He even challenged me to a bet that WMD were going to be found.

But our clash didn't come to a head until we added the Vietnam "oil" to the Iraq "flames." It happened over a movie, unfortunately a story that took place in Vietnam. Somewhere in the movie, a Vietnamese character said something to the effect that Americans did not need to be there. I voiced my agreement and said Americans did not need to be in Iraq, either. Visibly upset by my words and incensed by a nasty argument about to follow, my friend announced the get-together over. Soon after, our friendship was, too.

On the one hand, I was surprised by my friend's anger. By the time the Iraq War started, the United States had already had a normal diplomatic relationship with Vietnam for almost a decade, a bilateral trade agreement for several years, and a Vietnam War veteran as its ambassador to Hanoi. On

134

the other hand, I realized that with that anger I simply experienced decades later what I had missed out in this country: the hostile divide among Americans over the Vietnam War, now repeated over the Iraq War.

Just as the déjà vu of the anti-war and pro-war divide, there has also been déjà vu of the war ravages.

Now more than five years into the Iraq War, the death toll of American servicemen is over 4,000, the number of wounded is over 30,000, and the number of dead Iraqi civilians is into hundreds of thousands. Yet, no weapons of mass destruction have been found in Iraq. No freedom or liberty or peace or security has been gained for the Iraqis. All we have seen in Iraq is violence, chaos, destruction, misery, and with them, the continuing, and repeating, divide among Americans. How could I not think of the Chinese proverb again, with a big question mark this time: "Knowing today, wondering why yesterday?"

It is not just me that is wondering about the Iraq War. Kanan Makiya, a leading Iraqi intellectual in exile in America who more than any single person made the case for the American invasion of Iraq, has been wondering about the war, too. Comparing the number of deaths of Iraqis under Saddam Hussein and that since 2003, Mr. Makiya expressed regret, in early 2007 in *The New York Times*, regarding American policy there, "Everything they could do wrong, they did wrong."

I wonder more. I wonder if there is going to be an Iraq Veterans Memorial someday in Washington, D.C., with more names of American servicemen and servicewomen carved into marble. I wonder if Americans would learn the lesson of the Iraq War, if not the Vietnam War, and use it to remind another president against another futile war. I certainly wonder about my friend whom I lost to the other side of the great Iraq War divide. He has certainly lost the bet over the WMD in Iraq.

135

32. Politics Makes the Heart Grow Harder

Chinese saying: 人心都是肉长的
Pronunciation: Ren Xin Dou Shi Rou Zhang De
Translation: All Human Hearts Are Made of Flesh

What is suggested in the saying "All human hearts are made of flesh" is that all human beings have soft hearts and similar feelings. We all feel happy, sad, angry, etc., with our work, family, and struggle. We all feel pain over illness, injury, deaths, etc., among our fellow human beings.

But what we have in common with our hearts as human beings can change with politics. As we have seen in America in the first few years of the 21st century, when it comes to illness, injury, deaths, etc., brought by the Iraq War, what one feels seems to depend more on one's politics rather than his or her heart of flesh. The more one believes in the hard power of the war, the harder one's heart seems to grow.

That difference in hearts played out in a sensational way in the Congress in January 2007.

At a Senate hearing on President Bush's troop surge strategy, Sen. Barbara Boxer (D-CA) asked Secretary of State Condoleezza Rice a heart-felt question: "Who pays the price? I'm not going to pay a personal price. My kids are too old, and my grandchild is too young. You're not going to pay a price, as I understand it, within immediate family. So who pays the price? The American military and their families."

It was a very human question. It was about human lives, human families, and human sacrifices, or American lives, American families, and American sacrifices.

136

Rice, however, didn't see the question that way, even though she responded at the hearing that she fully understood the sacrifice that the American people, especially our soldiers, were making. As she later told the press, "In retrospect, gee, I thought single women had come further than that, that the only question is, 'Are you making good decisions because you have kids?'"

I was disheartened by Rice's counter questioning, especially the two words she used, "gee" and "good." That was when I remembered the saying in the title, "All human hearts are made of flesh," and realized how politics, war politics particularly, could make one's heart grow so hard.

"Good" in its normal sense is of course what we want for all people or the greatest number of people. But "good" in politics is as beauty in the eye of the beholder. The "good" Iraq War policy in the eye of Secretary Rice or President Bush was obviously not good for the majority of American voters who sent more Democrats to Congress in the 2006 mid-term election to express just that. It was certainly not good for those who had a son or daughter or husband or wife in Iraq, especially with a loved one returning from Iraq in a coffin. And it was opposite to good for the Iraqi people suffering and dying in the war zone.

The "gee" from Rice sounded so cold-hearted, even light-hearted, to such a heavy-hearted question as to who would pay the ultimate price for the prolonged Iraq War. I doubted Rice would have geed if she had an immediate family member serving in Iraq. It was as revealing that those with her in the administration or on the right attacked Boxer as being "outrageous" and making "a great leap backward for feminism." Together, they turned, purposely, a human issue, or a human heart issue, into one of women and feminism, of married women vs. single women, and of women with children vs. women without children, ignoring totally what Boxer was trying to do in the first place: bringing the focus of the Iraq policy debate to American families' sacrifice.

137

There have been many occasions in the duration of the Iraq War that reminded me of this Chinese saying about soft human hearts and showed me how politics could harden them.

I thought about the saying every Sunday when George Stephanopoulos on his ABC's *This Week* gave the list from the Pentagon of the American servicemen and servicewomen who had died in the past week, with their names, position, age, and hometowns. I tried to imagine what it was like for their families forever with an empty seat at the table and wondered if Secretary Rice ever felt bad reading those lists, if she did.

I thought about the saying each time I heard or saw news of Iraqi men, women and children blown up in their market place, mosques, schools, homes, cars, etc. by IEDs (improvised explosive devices) or by shots from American or allied patrols. I tried to imagine the broken life the Iraqi people had lived in the war and wondered if American politicians who supported the war had ever felt any sympathy with them.

I thought about the saying when I watched Mr. McLaughlin update weekly the human toll in Iraq during his show on PBS, especially on the Sept. 29-30 weekend of 2007 when he read out this: "U.S. military dead in Iraq, 3,801. One-half of those dead are 24 years of age and under." 24 and under?! I tried to imagine what those soldiers could have done in a normal life span with their education, love, career, etc. and wondered if President Bush, who had sent them to Iraq, ever stopped to think that they were as young as his own twin daughters.

I thought about the saying on Veterans Day 2007 when a National Alliance to End Homelessness study stated that half a million American veterans were homeless at some time during 2006, or one in four of the homeless population. Among them were veterans from the Vietnam War, the Gulf War and wars in Iraq and Afghanistan. I tried to imagine how sad the veterans must have been having risked their lives for their country overseas yet homeless at home and wondered if Vice President Cheney who talked most about supporting the troops ever noticed them on the street.

I thought about the saying when a five-month CBS research effort revealed in late 2007 the most tragic epidemic to date: at least 6,256 veterans had committed suicide in 2005 -- an average of 17 a day. Those soldiers had survived the battlefield but couldn't live with their mental illness, or "the severe psychological trauma after witnessing 'multiple dead' and having to 'sort through badly mutilated bodies'" as a CBS correspondent described. I tried to imagine the pain those soldiers' parents must have had in their hearts and wondered why our government let this happen.

I certainly thought about the saying when American military deaths reached 4,000 at the fifth anniversary of the Iraq War, when polls showed that two-thirds of Americans didn't think the war was worth it, especially when Vice President Cheney was asked about it and he said "So?" I couldn't believe it. What a heart of stone he had? I felt like shouting at him, with these questions:

Can our politicians behind the Iraq War still feel pain in their heart from so much human suffering, American as well as Iraqi, military as well as civilian?

Can or should a politician always put his or her politics above a fellow human being's or fellow citizen's life, not to say hundreds of thousands of those lives?

Should the most advanced country such as the United States still resort to wars and using human lives to revenge human lives to solve ideological differences with other countries in the 21st century?

After all, it is easy for politicians to talk about making sacrifices for a cause when they themselves do not have to. Maybe it would help if they learn this Chinese saying "All human hearts are made of flesh," and remember that all ultimate war sacrifices are human sacrifices. By keeping their hearts soft, whether they have children or not, they would make better decisions.

Or they could at least learn from Mao Zedong, the late Chinese communist leader and dictator, who had sent his own son Mao Anying to fight in the Korean War. The younger Mao died soon after arriving at the front, in an American air raid.

🐦   🐦   🐦   🐦   🐦

Part 4. U.S.-China Relations

33. The Balance of U.S.-China Relations

Chinese saying: 阴阳平衡
Pronunciation: Yin Yang Ping Heng
Translation: The Balance of Yin and Yang

According to China's Daoism, there are two primal forces, yin and yang, at play in the universe. Day and night, warm and cold, north and south, sun and moon, masculine and feminine, etc. are all pairs of yin and yang. As shown in the *taijitu*, or Diagram of the Supreme Ultimate, the black yin and white yang are the opposite two halves of the same circle. They chase each other, complement each other, reflect each other, and depend on each other. One can't exist without the other. Thus the theory of yin and yang: for everything to go well, its yin and yang have to be in balance. This is true in nature. This is true in human society. I would like to think that it is also true in relationships, I mean U.S.-China relations.

I still remember the disbelief and excitement I felt when I first heard, as a teenager back in China, that the Chinese government had invited American President Richard Nixon for a visit. I also remember a cousin's comment on China's brand new diplomatic relations with the U.S., "Wow, this is really some change. The Stars and Stripes used to stand for American imperialism, the enemy."

The normalization was really an unbelievable event. The U.S. and China were so different, so opposite and so hostile to each other that as a pair of yin and yang, instead of complementing each other, they repelled each other and could almost push each other out of the planet, if not the yin yang circle.

143

As American visitors to China always commented, especially after a tour to an emperor's tomb or a historical site, that China was so ancient, and America was so young.

They were right. China was one of the world's oldest civilizations while the United States was the new world. China had experienced defeat and invasion by foreign powers while the U.S. had triumphed from Independence War to Cold War. That was just history. The two were also different, extremely so, in every other way: China practiced socialism, with a centralized command economy while the U.S. practiced capitalism, with a free-market economy; China had a one-party communist government while the U.S. had a two-party democracy; China championed socialist and the Third World countries while the U.S. led the free world, etc. They were not only different and opposite; they were enemies.

However, all the differences and hostilities were put aside in 1972 by Mao and Nixon, who themselves being a great pair of yin and yang, in a quiet handshake that shook the world. The meeting and subsequent normalization was possible only because the two giants had found a balancing point between the two countries: their common concern over the growing threat of the Soviet Union.

President Nixon said after the meeting: "...we will build a bridge across sixteen thousand miles and twenty two years of hostility which have divided us in the past. Our two peoples tonight hold the future of the world in our hands."

More than three decades have passed since then. The "future" is here. But how is the "bridge" holding up? In other words, how is the balance of the relationship?

President Nixon would probably be pretty pleased with U.S.-China relations in general if he woke up today. As the world's two engines of economic growth, the two countries also share the largest amount of trade in the world. The U.S. no longer debates annually over China's Most Favored Nation trade status. Instead, it has welcomed China into the

World Trade Organization. The two countries have also been cooperating in a large number of areas, from counter-terrorism to nuclear security, from energy to environment.

However, President Nixon might also feel somewhat puzzled by a number of frictions existing today: the exploding U.S. trade deficit with China; Congress' frustration with China's currency value; U.S. concern over China's increasing reach around the world for resources and influence as well as its growing military capability and potential threat, etc.

But to President Nixon, the differences between the U.S. and China today should seem much more surmountable than in his time, and common ground would also seem much easier to find.

In the 1970s, for instance, the two countries had but one common interest, namely the international security concern over the Soviet Union. Yet, that was enough to have served very well as a balancing point in the relationship between the two hostile countries. Today, there are a large number of common interests between the U.S. and China and a broad range of cooperation, from trade to security, to serve as multiple and stronger balancing points in the relationship.

When you think about it, compared with the 1970s, the United States and China today make a much better pair of yin and yang. They remain very different but are also highly complementary. As the Chinese say, the U.S. is the largest developed country and China the largest developing country. They have a lot to offer each other and benefit from each other. In the Daoist light, they also need each other. The neocons may have been wrong to have believed China to be the next Soviet Union, but they were right in that the United States did need a balancing, if not countering, power in the world. After all, it takes yin and yang for the universe to go around—the complementary yin and yang, not the repelling ones.

145

When yin and yang are balanced, things will go well in our life. When the U.S. and China, the two great nations, are balanced in their relations, the world will be a better place.

34. Prison Labor in China and America

Chinese proverb: 五十步笑百步
Pronunciation: Wu Shi Bu Xiao Bai Bu
Translation: One Who Retreats Fifty Paces Mocking
One Who Retreats a Hundred

Prison labor, especially the Chinese prison labor, was a major topic as well as barrier in U.S.-China relations in the early 1990s. Former Chinese prisoner and naturalized American citizen Harry Wu wrote about it, testified in Congress about it, sneaked back in China to video-tape it, etc. He succeeded in making it big enough an issue for Congress to consider every year for a number of years before its vote on the Most Favored Nation trade status for China. Although President Clinton dropped in 1994 the linkage of China's trading status and its human rights record, prison labor had become a dirty word regardless of any context.

The debate over China's prisoners should have stayed focused on the issue of prisoners of conscience, not whether prisoners of all kinds, in China or the U.S., should do any work while serving time for their crimes at the cost of taxpayers. Everyone outside prison worked every day. Yet many of us seemed to expect our prisoners to enjoy prison as a retirement/entertainment/educational center fully equipped with television, computers, gym, library, college courses, plus, of course, free room and board, so that they could feel comfortable enough to think about their repentance?

But even if the debate was just about prison labor, the U.S. could have very well been, as in the title, the "One who retreats fifty paces mocking one who retreats a hundred."

The proverb came from the story of an ancient battle in China. During a fierce fighting, soldiers on one side began to

147

retreat. Some of them were faster than others. Those who had retreated about fifty paces laughed at those in front of them who had retreated about a hundred. The meaning of the proverb is close to that of the English saying, "The pot calling the kettle black."

When U.S. politicians talked about prison labor or prison-made products in China, they made it sound as if China was the only country on earth that had committed such an outrageous crime as to exploit innocent prisoners or violate their rights or freedom from forced labor. The fact was very different. As James Seymour and Richard Anderson pointed out in regard to their 1999 study, "New Ghosts, Old Ghosts: Prisons and Labor Reform Camps in China," most states in the U.S. required convicts to work, some even exported their products. The authors also stated that they didn't consider it either highly desirable or particularly evil for a prison to make a profit.

The United States routinely used prison labor during its early years as a republic. The practice was outlawed in 1930 by Congress, which passed a number of acts making it a felony to move prison goods across state borders. But prison labor didn't stop. Instead of making products for private businesses, inmates began making products for government agencies, license plates, for instance.

The situation changed again in the 1970s when Supreme Court Chief Justice Warren Burger pushed for turning prisons into "factories with fences." A good idea, I might add! He succeeded. In 1979, Congress lifted the ban on interstate transportation and sale of prison-made goods with laws such as the Justice System Improvement Act and programs such as the Prison Industries Enhancement Certification Program. Private industry got the green light and put prisoners back to work once more.

A simple search on the Internet would give one a pretty good idea on how a big business of "prison industries" had developed in the U.S. since then. There were "factories with fences" from Arizona to Washington, making products for or providing services to both public and private sectors. These products and services ranged from assembling furniture to washing police cars, from data entry to wiring schools to the Internet, from making garments to inspecting cosmetic containers, etc. Contractors for prison labor included Fortune 1,000 as well as federal and state government agencies.

The most interesting cases of prison labor included South Carolina inmates making lingerie for Victoria's Secret, Oregon inmates producing electronic menu boards for McDonald's, California inmates taking reservations over the phone during a flight attendants' strike, and Washington inmates wrapping software for Microsoft. It may sound horrible to some people, but to me it made all the sense, economically, socially, and humanely.

Another sticking point between the U.S. and China concerning prison labor was that China exported directly or indirectly some of its prison-made products to the American market. But while the U.S. was pointing the finger at China, prisons in California and Oregon were doing exactly the same: exporting their products, including the famous Prison Blues brand jeans to Asia, according to *Covert Action Quarterly*. The fact that U.S. had laws forbidding imports of prison products from other countries while it did not have laws regulating state prisons exporting their own products overseas was, of course, an interesting issue itself.

American prisons may have had better facilities than Chinese ones. American prisoners may also have had better pay for their work than Chinese prisoners. But when it came to using prison labor and exporting prison-made products, the difference between the United States and China was really one of degree, not nature. Therefore, the whole episode in the 1990s of the U.S. criticizing China of abusing prison labor and exporting prison-made products was simply, and truly, a case of "One who retreats fifty paces mocking one who retreats a hundred."

                🐦   🐦   🐦   🐦   🐦

35. U.S. Lenient with Itself on "Collateral Damage"

Chinese saying: 严以律己, 宽以待人
Pronunciation: Yan Yi Lu Ji, Kuan Yi Dai Ren
Translation: Strict with Oneself and Lenient towards Others

"Strict with oneself and lenient towards others" is one of the virtues touted in Chinese culture. What it suggests is that people should set a higher standard for themselves while showing more tolerance to others, or to be harder on themselves and easier on others.

Although it was mostly an advice for individuals in their behavior towards other people, it would be as good an advice for countries in their behavior towards other countries.

The United States has attached great importance of human rights in its foreign policy and has been very critical towards other countries, particularly China, on the issue. While the U.S. has put emphasis on freedom of speech and expression, China has argued that for a developing nation like itself, the rights to a reasonable living, adequate housing, universal education, etc. were as important. They were both right, considering the different stages of development each was in. But one right that should trump all others had to be the right to life, the most basic of human rights. That right was also famously written into the U.S. Declaration of Independence, along with liberty and pursuit of happiness.

One would think, and expect, that with its historical and Constitutional respect for human rights, the United States would hold itself to a very high standard in terms of safeguarding human lives under all circumstances. However, it occurred to me in the late 1990s it was not the case when it involved lives of foreign nationals.

151

From April to June 1999, for instance, during the NATO air strike led by the United States in Yugoslavia, mistaken bombs dropped on buses, trains, refugee caravans, apartments, and markets and killed hundreds to thousands of Yugoslav civilians and injured more. In addition, a large number of hospitals, schools, factories, power plants, bridges, railways, highways, and civilian airports were also destroyed in the same way. Yet, American as well as NATO leaders simply, and conveniently, called all those civilian deaths and destruction "collateral damage."

One couldn't help wondering: Didn't those Yugoslavs have parents and children, husbands and wives, sisters and brothers, just as Americans did? Did they lose their basic human rights, the right to life, because of the crimes of their leader Milosevic? Did any American politicians and human rights leaders lose any sleep over them?

Further more, during the same period, NATO mistakenly, again, as was explained, slammed three missiles into the Chinese Embassy in Belgrade, killing three and wounding over 20, bringing the atrocity by NATO's errors to a new height.

What was more incomprehensible was the fact that after the deadly Chinese embassy bombing, no prompt statement with contrition came from the U.S. government or NATO. An apology did come reluctantly in the end from President Clinton. But it was given not at a special press conference, not with any special arrangement, but as an afterthought during a busy political fund-raising trip. It also didn't come until after waves of angry protest had swept China and after repeated demands from the Chinese government. It was obvious that it came out of pressure from China, not of U.S.'s own initiative.

One couldn't help wondering. Even if the Chinese government may have condoned some of the violent protests against the NATO bombing, and the human rights record of the same government had been less than good, didn't the Chinese people, as people anywhere, who suffered loss of loved ones because of a NATO mistake, deserve sincere apologies as well as compensation? Imagine if it had been an American embassy that had been bombed and American citizens that had been killed and injured by a China-led international force and be dismissed simply as "collateral damage."

In a number of television interviews following the embassy bombing with Li Zhaoxing, then Chinese Ambassador to the United States, the first question the hosts asked was whether American personnel were safe in China. The Ambassador was clearly, and rightly, disappointed. Where was any concern for the Chinese personnel just killed or injured and their families coping with the sudden loss, the ambassador asked back.

In contrast, after the capture of three American soldiers by the Yugoslav military, President Clinton delivered a strong protest and threat, rightly, of course. American media also gave full coverage to the soldiers for days and conducted interviews with the families across television channels. All the while, however, the soldiers' lives were never in danger and were released in a month.

But did we see any coverage of the Yugoslav civilian casualties and families or the Chinese casualties and families? No. "Americans stifle a yawn as U.S. pilots rain terror," read the title of a syndicated column, capturing the American reaction, or lack of it, towards lives lost of other peoples as a result of American doing. The questions begged asking were: Was an American life worth more than a Yugoslav or Chinese one? Was the respect of human life more of a demand on other countries than on the U.S. itself? What happened to the belief that all men were created equal?

To me, regarding the loss of Yugoslav and Chinese lives as mere "collateral damage" seemed to be a case where the U.S. was strict with others in terms of human rights while lenient towards itself. It seemed also a case where the U.S. talked the talk of human rights while not walked the walk of human rights.

"Strict with oneself and lenient towards others" is not an easy thing to do. That is why it is a virtue. But setting a good example for others to follow is always better than telling others what to do, in human rights or in any other areas.

36. The Upside Down View on Taiwan

Chinese proverb: 本末倒置
Pronunciation: Ben Mo Dao Zhi
Translation: Taking the Branch for the Root

In my life as a Chinese citizen, Taiwan was really not that big an issue. It was an old one, of course: a province temporarily controlled by those corrupt, incompetent and doomed Nationalists who had fled the mainland after losing the civil war to the Communists; a "running dog of the American imperialists" with financial and military support from the United States; an island that belonged to China and would be re-unified with the mainland sooner or later, etc.

When the United States and China were normalizing their diplomatic relations in the late 1970s, Taiwan became a big issue, or a big barrier. Fortunately, the two sides worked it out. In the famous "Three Joint Communiqués," they agreed that the U.S. recognized the government of the People's Republic of China as the sole legal government of China; the U.S. acknowledged the Chinese position that there was but one China and Taiwan was part of China; the U.S. did not challenge that position; it did not seek to carry out a long-term policy of arms sales to Taiwan, and it intended gradually to reduce its sales of arms to Taiwan, leading, over a period of time, to a final resolution.

That was a very good compromise. But that was about as far as my thought on Taiwan went. I didn't follow the Taiwan issue much beyond that, even after I came to be on the U.S. side of the U.S.-China relations. It, however, followed me.

At the invitation of two friends, I went to a Chinese cultural event in Atlanta in the late 1980s. To my surprise, the national anthem of Taiwan was being played. Only then did I

155

realize that it was a Taiwan event. People were standing up, including my friends! No, not me, a mainland Chinese, from a family of veteran communists, no way…Half way into the music, however, sort of seeking a "middle ground," I stood up briefly, with great discomfort, for the sake of my friends and maybe the ultimate reunification of China as well. It was a great relief when the music ended. My friends, who were non-Chinese, didn't sense anything wrong.

Visiting my doctor's office one day in a Seattle suburb in the mid 1990s, I was asked about my family medical history. To the question of place of residence of my parents, I simply answered, "China." "Which China?" my doctor came back. I was a little surprised, but more amused. "There is only one China, doctor," I said with a smile. But my doctor, who was very kind and friendly, was ready to retreat, saying: "I wouldn't touch that with a 10-foot pole." OK, doc, I said in my head.

During Christmas holiday one year in the late 1990s, I had guests over for dinner. Even though we had never thought of discussing anything political, we somehow bumped into Taiwan. One of the guests, a former navy officer who had been stationed for many years in East Asia, expressed great admiration for Taiwan. His said in effect that he was very impressed that the little guy, meaning Taiwan, could stand up to the big guy, meaning mainland China. I didn't respond much. It was Christmas after all.

My friends at the Atlanta event, my doctor, and the ex-navy officer at my dinner were pretty representative of Americans' views on Taiwan. They clearly saw China and Taiwan separately. They could obviously get along with both China and Taiwan. But at the same time, they naturally sympathized with and rooted for Taiwan the "little guy" against China the "big guy."

Their understanding, or misunderstanding, was enhanced in 2000 by a bill passed in Congress called the Taiwan Security Enhancement Act. As an update to the Taiwan Relations Act of 1979 that had defined the unofficial relationship with Taiwan upon normalization of U.S.-China relations, the new bill provided for further U.S. military relations with Taiwan as well as continued U.S. support for Taiwan to protect itself from coercion and use of force against it. By whom? By the big and bullying China, of course. Oh, poor little Taiwan.

I realized that the Taiwan issue had become backwards, or upside down, in the United States. I was not sure if it was a case of "Putting the cart before the horse," but I was pretty sure that it was one of "Taking the branch for the root," as the Chinese proverb in the title said, meaning the emphasis was wrong.

To many Americans, Taiwan may have indeed seemed small and innocent against the huge and unyielding China. But they may not know that things hadn't always been that way. In fact, things had been the other way round. The Nationalists on Taiwan used to be the big guy in power in China, while the Communists, or "communist bandits," were the little guy. Not only were they big, the Nationalists also had a big friend in the United States. American support had come in the form of hundreds of millions of dollars plus weapons, aircraft, trucks, etc. But alas, Nationalists the big guy lost the civil war to Communists the little guy, fled the mainland to the island province called Taiwan, and became the "little guy." Even though Taiwan has evolved into a democracy since then, the Taiwan issue has never been one of China bullying Taiwan. Taiwan being the "little guy" today is more a result of Nationalists' defeat on the mainland over half a century before, plus its natural geographic position, than anything else.

It should be pretty clear that the Taiwan issue was a leftover from the Chinese civil war. It became a big issue between the United States and China because of two simple facts: China wanted to settle the score of its civil war; the U.S.

157

wasn't able to get over its loss, or the Nationalists' loss, of China.

If you still do not quite appreciate China's firm stand on re-unifying Taiwan without third party interference, this little analogy of an imaginary Republic of America might help:

> The ruling Republicans and the insurgent Democrats were fighting a civil war. The Republicans lost, fled to the island state called Hawaii, took the remnant American government there, and vowed to return to the mainland. The Democrats established the People's Republic of America, set up a new American government in Washington D.C. and declared that Hawaii was part of America and would be re-unified sooner or later. China had supported the Republicans during the war, refused to recognize the new American government, and continued its official ties with the Republicans on Hawaii. Years passed. Out of geopolitical needs, China normalized its diplomatic relations with the People's Republic of America represented by the Democratic government in DC and switched its relations with Hawaii to unofficial. Seeing no hope of taking the continental America back, the Hawaiian government decided to try independence. The Democratic American government said no way. Meanwhile, China has continued to support Hawaii, with a Hawaii Security Enhancement Act and arms sales, etc.

The "Hawaii" issue in this analogy was really one between the Americans themselves, with no need of interference from China. It was a leftover from the American "civil war," not one of mainland America the big guy bullying Hawaii the little guy. There should be no "two Americas," or "one America, one Hawaii," because Hawaii was part of America.

As only logical and reasonable, that was also what the United States agreed to with China: no infringing on Chinese sovereignty and territorial integrity, or interfering in China's internal affairs, or pursuing a policy of "two Chinas" or "one

158

China, one Taiwan," and with an interest in a peaceful settlement of the Taiwan issue by the Chinese themselves.

In a word, branch is branch and root is root. They shouldn't be confused.

37. Suspecting China of Being America's Enemy

Chinese proverb: 疑人偷斧
Pronunciation: Yi Ren Tou Fu
Translation: Suspecting Neighbor of Stealing One's Ax

Once upon a time, there was a man who owned an ax. One day, he couldn't find it anywhere. He suspected that his neighbor had stolen it. He began to watch the neighbor carefully, the way the neighbor walked, talked, and smiled. The more he watched, the more suspicious he became, and the more the neighbor looked liked a thief. Then he stumbled upon the ax himself. He had simply misplaced it. He watched the neighbor again, as carefully. Now the neighbor no longer looked like a thief, the way the neighbor walked, talked, and smiled.

That was the story behind the Chinese proverb in the title. It described how suspicions could influence and even become our beliefs.

One group of people that reminded me a lot of this proverb was the Blue Team, a camp of China watchers in the United States. As the opposite of the Red Team that favored a cooperative relationship with China, the Blue Team viewed China as the second Soviet Union bent on burying the United States.

The late 1990s was a busy time for the Blue Team. They published a number of books promoting fear of China among the American public. There was, for instance, *Year of the Rat*, on the danger of appeasement of President Clinton's China policy; *Red Dragon Rising*, on China's frightening military build-up and expansion; *The Coming Conflict with China*, on the inevitability of the rivalry and war between China and the United States, etc. They pushed through from behind the

160

scene the House bill named Taiwan Security Enhancement Act to strengthen military ties with Taiwan. They cheered for the Cox Report by a House select committee charging China of stealing nuclear weapon technologies from the United States. They watched with a hidden glee in early 2001 when a U.S. spy plane and a Chinese fighter collided over the South China Sea, in anticipation that the accident might evolve into a crisis, or even a conflict, between the U.S. and China that they had been predicting all along.

But suspicions were just that, suspicions, unfounded. People grew suspicious when they did not have sufficient knowledge and information about something and let their assumptions and imaginations run wild. That was the case with the man who was looking for his ax. That was also the case with the Blue Team, whose members were looking for an enemy for the U.S. in the post-Cold War era. The more the man was suspicious of his neighbor, the more the neighbor looked like a thief. The more the Blue Team was suspicious of China, the more China looked like an enemy to the United States.

Alas, 9/11 took place. The biggest, and real, threat to the United States turned out not to be China but the radical Islamic terrorist groups that were truly bent on burying the United States. I wondered how members of the Blue Team felt upon learning that the Islamic terrorists flew airplanes into the World Trade Center in New York and the Pentagon. They must have felt at least as stupid as the man stumbling onto the ax he had misplaced himself. The Blue Team had simply misplaced their target for an enemy.

But suspicions did not only grow out of a lack of knowledge and information; they could also be the result of misconception and bias. With vast differences between the U.S. and China, a great deal of bias and misconception had existed in American and Chinese understandings of each other, with a wealth of suspicions.

161

For instance, when the American-led NATO forces bombed the Chinese Embassy in Yugoslavia on May 8, 1999, angry protests swept across 20 cities in China. American Ambassador James Sasser was trapped inside the American Embassy in Beijing for days while demonstrators threw stones outside. The Chinese were outraged, first of all, because of the attack on China's sovereignty along with Chinese casualties. They were also indignant because of what they suspected to be the American intent: a punishment of China's past support of Yugoslav leader Milosevic; displeasure at China's opposition to the NATO bombing campaign in Yugoslavia; a test of the Chinese people's willpower and response in a potential conflict with the U.S.; an attempt to alert the Chinese of the tenth anniversary of the 1989 Tiananmen tragedy; a show of force as a warning to China in any possible move against Taiwan; etc. The delay of an explanation from the U.S. and NATO didn't help the situation.

But the tension began to ease after President Clinton offered his apology for the bombing in a phone call as well as a letter to Chinese President Jiang Zemin. NATO called the bombing a tragic error caused by outdated maps. The U.S. government agreed to pay the damages to China, too. With that, the mass anger in China based on suspicions subsided.

On April 1, 2001, a U.S. navy spy plane flying over the South China Sea came within 80 miles of China's Hainan province. A Chinese fighter jet intercepted it. A collision occurred. The Chinese fighter crashed into the sea, with the pilot killed. The American spy plane made an emergency landing inside Hainan.

Yet, before all the details were out, hardliners in America were already accusing China of being aggressive. President Bush, fresh from assuming the presidency, was eager to show his hawkishness towards China to distinguish himself from Clinton. In his first statement on the emergency, President Bush demanded prompt return of the crew and the plane from the Chinese government as if the Chinese had kid-

napped the Americans. When the Chinese side was still inves-
tigating the case, and with American diplomats having already
met with the crew, Rep. Henry Hyde (R-IL), the late chairman of the House International Relations Committee, was
already calling the crew hostages. All the bellicosity had, of
course, come from the suspicions of the Blue Team crowd:
that it was a calculated and crude provocation by the Chinese
communists aimed at bullying President Bush into not selling
defensive weapons to Taiwan; it was the expanding Chinese
military testing the limits of a confrontation with the United
States; it was China showing its nationalist hubris; it was the
Chinese President Jiang Zemin who needed the jingoism with
Washington for power struggle inside China; and, additionally,
it was the Chinese playing the blame game with the U.S. to
cover their own failures at home, etc.

Deflating all the unnecessary hostilities, Tony Karon of
Time magazine offered this brilliant scenario:

> "Imagine a Chinese plane flying a surveillance mission
> off the Florida coast colliding with a Navy F-16 sent on
> an aggressive monitoring mission. The Navy fighter goes
> down and the pilot is lost; the Chinese plane is forced to
> land on U.S. soil. The incident occurs at a moment when
> China is about to supply a package of sophisticated
> weapons to Cuba..."

In the end, the U.S. government said very sorry for the death
of the Chinese pilot and apologized for the spy plane's entering of the Chinese airspace and landing in Hainan without
authorization. The American crew returned home, too, safe
and sound. President Bush later praised Secretary of State
Colin Powell for his help in the calm diplomatic handling of
the incident, avoiding a possible crisis in U.S.-China relations.

One could see from the above examples that suspicions
could be pretty stupid. They also always made things worse.

163

"Suspecting neighbor of stealing one's ax" may be a simple story, but it has a very important lesson: when faced with a less than fully-understood or less than expected turn of event, it would be better if we take a deep breath and find out as much information as possible before jumping to any conclusion based on suspicions out of our own ignorance, misconception, or bias. Or you may just risk making a fool of yourself, as our Blue Team friends did.

❦ ❦ ❦ ❦ ❦

38. China's Human Rights Practice vs. America's Racial Record

Chinese saying: 风物常宜放眼量
Pronunciation: Feng Wu Chang Yi Fang Yan Liang
Translation: Things Are Better Seen in Perspective

The Chinese saying above in fact came from a poem written by Mao Zedong for a friend. It formed the second part of this couplet: "Too many grievances cause heartbreaks; things are better seen in perspective."

For whatever reason Mao wrote that poem, the advice on perspective became a popular saying in China. It has been used to suggest that events in life, positive and negative, past and present, are not isolated, but related. Therefore they should be looked upon together in perspective.

Indeed. Nothing stands alone. Everything is related to everything else. Things also constantly change. A good perspective is necessary for an individual or a country, in personal matters or international matters. But perspective is oftentimes forgotten.

The human rights issue, for instance, has been a focus of tension between the United States and China for a long time. It was over China's human rights practice that Congress debated annually for twenty some years before each renewal of the MFN (Most Favored Nation) trade status for China. It was because of China's human rights practice that many in the U.S., from congressmen and congresswomen to men and women in the street, opposed China's entry into the WTO (World Trade Organization). It has also been China's human rights practice that the State Department criticizes annually in its report to Congress.

165

Human rights issue of a country is of course very important, but it is not an isolated issue. It has to do with a country's history, culture, politics, economy, and especially its level of development. Countries at different stages of development have different levels of human rights. Developed countries always have better human rights than developing countries. Even within the same country, human rights in its post-industrial era are always better than they were in its industrial and pre-industrial eras. Take the United States itself as an example:

As we all know, the predecessor of the WTO was the GATT (General Agreement of Tariffs and Trade). If you check briefly into the history of the GATT, you will find that it originated from a U.N. Conference on Trade and Employment in Cuba in 1946. The conference had been held to consider a proposal by the United States and the United Kingdom on the establishment of an international trade organization. The new organization did not materialize, but the trade negotiations brought the GATT into being in 1947. The United States was, of course, one of its 23 original signatories. But what did that have anything to do with this discussion?

As we all know, the notorious Jim Crow Laws were in place in southern states of the United States for almost a century, from 1876 to 1965. The so-called "separate but equal" laws restricted the use by blacks of public schools, public transportation, and public accommodations, such as hotels, restaurants and recreational facilities. Only in 1954, with the landmark case of Brown vs. Board of Education, did the Supreme Court declare the segregation of public schools unconstitutional. Only in 1955 and 1956, after the defiant bus ride by Rosa Parks and the Montgomery Bus Boycott led by Rev. Martin Luther King, Jr. respectively, did the practice of bus segregation begin to end. Only in 1964, with the passage of the Civil Rights Act, did racial segregation as well as discrimination based on race, color, religion, sex, or national origin in public facilities, in government, and in employment, etc., become illegal. And only in the early 1970s did the segregation of public schools actually come to an end.

As many of us also know that it was in December 1948 that the Universal Declaration of Human Rights was adopted by the General Assembly of the United Nations, of which the United States was a charter member. Article One of that Declaration had this statement, "All human beings are born free and equal in dignity and rights. They are endowed with reason and conscience and should act towards one another in a spirit of brotherhood." 1948? But in America, there were still public drinking fountains marked "White" and "Colored"...

So the questions were obvious: Between 1948 when the Universal Declaration of Human Rights was adopted and 1964 when the Civil Rights Act became law, what would you say about the human rights in the United States? Between 1947 when the GATT was established and the 1970s when public school segregation in America finally ended, what would you say about the fact that other GATT member countries had been trading with an officially racist United States?

From that racial experience of America's own, we could see how human rights evolved with the development of the American society. Likewise, we should also try to see that human rights evolve as well with the development of the Chinese society. However, the two countries are very different, in political system and in level of development, and it is not always parallel to compare the practice of human rights. Take for example health care.

With the increasing number of Americans without health insurance in recent years, at 47 million in 2007, American politicians, physicians and non-government organizations have begun to talk about a new right for Americans: the right to health care. Sen. Hillary Clinton, during her presidential campaigning in 2008, called universal health care a human

167

right, not a privilege that was given and taken away. Others even called it an unalienable right, as the right to education.

So if health care was a human right, here is an ironic twist regarding China. Before the economic reforms, China used to provide its citizens, urban citizens at least, with cradle-to-grave welfare, including free medical care, along with free education, lifetime employment, pension, etc. It was called the "iron rice bowl." Alas, the Chinese broke that "bowl" when they embarked on the road of a market-oriented economy. However, in the new economic era, the fledgling social security and health care programs have left many Chinese without health care coverage. So would you say that the Chinese citizens enjoyed better human rights before the reforms than after, even than those Americans without health insurance now?

I am not sure what would be the answer to that question. But I think this Chinese saying would be helpful: Things are better seen in perspective. It is true. Things do become clearer in perspective, vertical and horizontal, economic and political, cultural and historical.

In perspective, one could see how much the United States has changed from its pre-civil rights movement days to today. In perspective, one could also see that for a country as ancient as China, fifty some years as the People's Republic was but one quick bend in a long river of history. The reforms of three decades haven't made China perfect. The Chinese society is also far from being free. But the Chinese people today are definitely freer, freer not only than all the generations before them, but also than those Americans who had to fight for their right to sit where they wanted in a public bus.

39. Look at the Forest of China, Not Just a Few Trees

Chinese proverb: 只见树木, 不见森林
Pronunciation: Zhi Jian Shu Mu, Bu Jian Sen Lin
Translation: Seeing Trees Only, But Not the Forest

As one of the more popular Chinese proverbs, this one suggests that when you see trees only, but not the forest, you are being partial rather than impartial, and you are seeing only part of a picture rather than the whole picture.

It seems a simple concept that one should always see the whole picture of an issue, an event, a development, etc., but it is not always an easy thing to do.

For a country as big and complicated as China, it is even harder, if not impossible, to see the whole picture of its many issues, events, developments, etc., especially when there are different views or biases involved. Here are a few cases of "seeing trees only," in my eyes, of the well known China stories over the years. I am not claiming to know the whole picture myself, just try to add a few trees to the understanding.

One-child policy: Many Americans, for instance, have a very negative view about China's one-child family policy, calling it draconian, inhumane, etc. They probably did not, however, have an idea, or experience, of what it was like to live in or govern a country with over 20% of the world's population, or to feed over a billion people with mere 7% of the world's arable land, or provide all necessary social services for everybody, or to create enough jobs each year for millions entering the work force, etc. They probably also did not know that the one-child policy was only for the Han Chinese, the majority of the Chinese population, and only those in urban areas, too. China's minority ethnic groups, numbering more than 50, including Tibetans, Mongolians, Uygurs, Huis, Zhuangs, etc., have been either exempt or given preferential quotas from the time the one-child policy was adopted in the late 1970s. As a result, the population of minorities has grown faster than the Han population. The rural Chinese, more than two-thirds of the population, have always been allowed to have two children or more.

Falun Gong: Many Americans have felt sympathetic towards *Falun Gong*, seeing it as an innocent and spiritual exercise group. They probably did not, however, know that it had reportedly caused as many as 1,500 people to die by the time it was banned in China in 1999. Those deaths resulted either from members refusing medical treatment or from murder by other members, all in the name of following the founder Li Hongzhi's doomsday teachings. That was more than the 39 members of the Heaven's Gate who committed suicide in 1997; more than the 86 members who lost their lives in the Branch Davidian fire in Waco, Texas in 1993; and even more than the 900 members of the People's Temple who died in mass "revolutionary suicide" under the instruction of its leader Jim Jones. It may be one thing to practice *qi gong*, or breathing exercise, but it was quite another to have practitioners kill themselves or others in order to elevate to the "next world."

"Sweatshops": Many Americans have heard stories of how some of China's factories were "sweatshops," thinking that the Chinese government was exploiting workers. They probably did not, however, learn that those "sweatshops" were often owned and operated by non-mainland Chinese companies and contracted by American companies. One typical case in the late 1990s, for instance, involved Nike, the shoe giant, criticized for its labor practices in hundreds of its contract factories in China and Southeast Asia. The exposure prompted Nike to improve conditions in those "sweatshops." Along with the "sweatshop," many in America have also complained about China's cheap labor. They probably did not, however, consider that when a country was industrializing and trading with industrialized countries, its "selling" point, or its comparative advantage, was its low-cost labor. If the Chinese workers had working conditions and compensation packages similar to those of American workers, there might not have been much China trade, or many Americans who could afford Nike shoes.

Religious beliefs: Many Americans, especially if they are Christian, have had the impression that religious activities in China were not as free as in the U.S. They probably did not, however, realize that China was not as religious a country as the U.S. in the first place. The majority of Chinese have always been atheists. Over the last few decades, however, the number of believers in China has grown impressively along with the country's economy. According to a survey by East China Normal University in 2005-06, the total number of believers in China was at 300 million strong. Besides, Christianity was only one of the religions followed there. Of China's total religious population, about 40 million were Christians, while more than 200 million were Buddhists, Daoists or worshippers of legendary figures such as the Dragon King and God of Fortune, etc. 300 million believers! That's about the size of the U.S. population. And the number is still growing.

Human rights: Most Americans, of course, have become familiar with the criticisms of China's human rights practice, especially political rights. They probably have never, however, heard of the many newfound rights the Chinese citizens now enjoy that they never had before: consumer rights, property rights, labor rights, investor rights, medical rights, marital rights, etc. Before the reforms, for instance, the Chinese were not able even to change their jobs or place of residence freely, or marry or divorce without the approval from their employers, or travel overseas or even keep correspondence with friends overseas, or own any business or property, etc. Now they can do all these and more, much more.

171

Human rights are also not only political rights. Since "Everyone has the right to a standard of living adequate for the health and well-being of himself and of his family…" as stated in the Universal Declaration of Human Rights, the most significant progress in human rights in China has to be the improvement of Chinese citizens' living standard. In 1978 when China first started its Reform and Opening Up program, there were 250 million rural Chinese living in poverty. 30 years later, in 2008, that number was down to 15 million. That was a world record in poverty reduction, both by rate and scale, according to the World Bank.

All in all, China, as a forest, has millions upon millions of trees of all kinds, sizes and annual rings. You may have seen a few of them, even crooked ones at that. Step back a little, you might get a better view. Step back some more, you would see a grand forest.

இ   இ   இ   இ   இ

Afterword

First of all, I would like to thank you, dear reader, for checking out this book of mine.

Becoming an American, I realize, is one thing, but understanding America is quite another. At the same time, I am sure you agree that being an American also means being free to think, and express, differently, from whatever angle.

I would also like to thank all those who have given me their friendship over the years in America, who have shared with me their thoughts on various issues, and especially those who have encouraged and helped me along with my writing effort. A special thank-you goes to Bruce Ramsey, editorial writer at *The Seattle Times*, for reading the draft of this book and making valuable suggestions.

What better way to close this book than with another Chinese proverb: Caste a brick to attract jade.

My book is, of course, the brick, and your comments and feedback, the jade.

Wendy Liu

July 2007 (First draft)

October 2008 (Final draft)

Homa & Sekey Books Titles on China

September's Fable: A Novel
By Zhang Wei. Trans. by Terrence Russell & Shawn X. Ye
Order No 1050, ISBN-10: 1931907463, ISBN-13: 9781931907460
Paperback, 6 x 9, 495p, 2007, $29.95, Fiction

September's Fable tells the story of the rise and fall of a Chinese coastal village through its difficult formation, hard existence and inevitable disintegration. Spanning approximately sixty years, the novel is a rich and intriguing tapestry of life and death in rural China. Somewhat in the tradition of William Faulkner and Gabriel García Márquez, September's Fable weaves history, politics, and folklore close together to bring an enchanting way of storytelling that dexterously touches on such universal themes as love and hate, war and revolution, city and country, the noble and the ugly, and, more importantly, the inevitability of the old superseded by the new and young.

Journey across the Four Seas: A Chinese Woman's Search for Home By Veronica Li
Order No: 1047, ISBN: 1931907439, Paperback, 6 x 9, 298p, 2007, $14.95, Nonfiction/Memoir

This is a true and touching story of one Chinese woman's search for home. It is also an inspiring book about human yearning for a better life. To escape poverty, Flora Li fought her way through the education system and became one of the few women to get into the prestigious Hong Kong University. Throughout her migrations, from Shanghai to Nanking to Hong Kong to Bangkok to Taipei and finally across the four seas to the U.S., Flora kept her sight on one goal—providing her children with the best possible education.

The Holy Spark: Rogel and the Goddess of Liberty
By Yu Li, Trans. by Haiyan Chen & Xianfeng Mu
Order No 1046, ISBN 1931907420, Hardcover, 6 x 9, 260p, 2006, $16.99, Fiction

"*The Holy Spark* is a splendid novel in the great tradition of *Alice in Wonderland, The Wonderful Wizard of Oz,* and *The Chronicles of Narnia.* It is perfect for young readers and will keep them highly entertained for hours."
— **Barry Moreno, historian and author, Statue of Liberty & Ellis Island Museum**

Homa & Sekey Books Titles on China

The Haier Way: The Making of a Chinese Business Leader and a Global Brand By Jeannie J. Yi, PhD & Shawn X. Ye, MBA
Order No 1009, ISBN: 1-931907-01-3, Hardcover, Business, $24.95

Haier is the largest consumer appliance maker in China. The book traces the appliance giant's path to success, from its early bleak years to becoming the world's 5th largest household appliance manufacturer. The book explains how Haier excelled in quality, service, technology innovation, a global vision and a management style that is a blend of Jack Welch of "GE" and Confucius of ancient China.

I enjoyed reading through it – A great story! Haier is certainly an impressive company.

— **Jack Welch**, former GE Chairman and CEO

China's Generation Y:
Understanding the Future Leaders of the World's Next Superpower
By Michael Stanat, United Nations International School
Order No 1029, ISBN 1931907250, Hardcover, 6 x 9, 222 pp., $24.95
Order No 1040, ISBN 1931907323, Paperback, 6 x 9, 222 pp., $17.95
Contemporary Affairs, 2006

Based upon interviews and surveys conducted in Shanghai by the author, this is the first English book to look into all aspects of China's young generation — their life styles, relationships with family and society, views, dreams and development... *China's Generation Y* provides a rare glimpse into the lives and minds of today's youth and tomorrow's leaders, showing Western readers who they are, how they got there, and where they are headed.

Paintings by Xu Jin: Tradition and Innovation in Chinese Fine Brushwork. Preface by Prof. Robert E. Harrist, Jr., Columbia University, Order No 1028, ISBN 1931907234, Hardcover, 10½ x 10½, 128pp., color illustrations throughout, $39.50, Art

This book brings together over seventy Chinese fine brushwork paintings by Xu Jin, including figures, landscapes, animals, flowers and birds. Drawing on sources in earlier art and traditional iconography, Xu Jin's paintings are characterized by stylish composition, impressive colors, and fine lines. They not only demonstrate a natural integration of verse, calligraphy, painting and seal, but also a fine combination of Chinese and Western painting skills.

Homa & Sekey Books Titles on China

Willow Leaf, Maple Leaf: A Novel of Immigration Blues
By David Ke, PhD, Order No 1036, ISBN: 1931907242, 5 ½ x 8 ½,
Paperback, 2006, 203 pp., $16.95 Fiction/Asian-American Studies

Willow Leaf is a dazzlingly beautiful Chinese woman who is smuggled
to Canada. While working at a sweatshop and at a massage parlor—and
through several extramarital affairs—she learns that survival in a different country might mean a compromise of morals. Eventually, she finds
new wealth and new love with an elderly man and has her own successful business. But can Willow Leaf truly leave her love for her family and
China behind?

Flower Terror: Suffocating Stories of China by Pu Ning
ISBN 0-9665421-0-X, Fiction, Paperback, $13.95

"The stories in this work are well written." **– Library Journal**

Acclaimed Chinese writer eloquently describes the oppression of
intellectuals in his country between 1950s and 1970s in these twelve
autobiographical novellas and short stories. Many of the stories are so
shocking and heart-wrenching that one cannot but feel suffocated.

The Peony Pavilion: A Novel by Xiaoping Yen, PhD
ISBN 0-9665421-2-6, Fiction, Paperback, $16.95

"A window into the Chinese literary imagination." **– Publishers Weekly**

A sixteen-year-old girl visits a forbidden garden and falls in love with a
young man she meets in a dream. She has an affair with her dream-lover
and dies longing for him. After her death, her unflagging spirit continues
to wait for her dream-lover. Does her lover really exist? Can a youthful
love born of a garden dream ever blossom? The novel is based on a
sixteenth-century Chinese opera written by Tang Xianzu, "the
Shakespeare of China."

Butterfly Lovers: A Tale of the Chinese Romeo and Juliet
By Fan Dai, PhD, ISBN 0-9665421-4-2, Fiction, Paperback, $16.95

"An engaging, compelling, deeply moving, highly recommended and
rewarding novel." **– Midwest Books Review**

A beautiful girl disguises herself as a man and lives under one roof with
a young male scholar for three years without revealing her true identity.
They become sworn brothers, soul mates and lovers. In a world in which
marriage is determined by social status and arranged by parents, what is
their inescapable fate?

Homa & Sekey Books Titles on China

The Dream of the Red Chamber: An Allegory of Love
By Jeannie Jinsheng Yi, PhD, ISBN: 0-9665421-7-7, Hardcover
Asian Studies/Literary Criticism, $49.95

Although dreams have been studied in great depth about this most influential classic Chinese fiction, the study of all the dreams as a sequence and in relation to their structural functions in the allegory is undertaken here for the first time.

Always Bright: Paintings by American Chinese Artists 1970-1999
Edited by Xue Jian Xin et al.
ISBN 0-9665421-3-4, Art, Hardcover, $49.95

"An important, groundbreaking, seminal work." **–Midwest Book Review**

A selection of paintings by eighty acclaimed American Chinese artists in the late 20th century, *Always Bright* is the first of its kind in English publication. The album falls into three categories: oil painting, Chinese painting and other media painting. It also offers profiles of the artists and information on their professional accomplishment.

Always Bright, Vol. II: Paintings by Chinese American Artists
Edited by Eugene Wang, Harvard Univ., et al.
ISBN: 0-9665421-6-9, Art, Hardcover, $50.00

A sequel to the above, the book includes artworks of ninety-two artists in oil painting, Chinese painting, watercolor painting, and other media such as mixed media, acrylic, pastel, pen and pencil, etc. The book also provides information on the artists and their professional accomplishment. Artists included come from different backgrounds, use different media and belong to different schools. Some of them enjoy international fame while others are enterprising young men and women who are more impressionable to novelty and singularity.

Musical Qigong: Ancient Chinese Healing Art from a Modern Master
By Shen Wu, ISBN: 0-9665421-5-0, Health, Paperback, $14.95

Musical Qigong is a special healing energy therapy that combines two ancient Chinese traditions-healing music and Qigong. This guide contains two complete sets of exercises with photo illustrations and discusses how musical Qigong is related to the five elements in the ancient Chinese concept of the universe - metal, wood, water, fire, and earth.

Homa & Sekey Books Titles on China

Ink Paintings by Gao Xingjian, the Nobel Prize Winner
ISBN: 1-931907-03-X, Hardcover, Art, $34.95

An extraordinary art book by the Nobel Prize Winner for Literature in 2000, this volume brings together over sixty ink paintings by Gao Xingjian that are characteristic of his philosophy and painting style. Gao believes that the world cannot be explained, and the images in his paintings reveal the black-and-white inner world that underlies the complexity of human existence. People admire his meditative images and evocative atmosphere by which Gao intends his viewers to visualize the human conditions in extremity.

Splendor of Tibet: The Potala Palace, Jewel of the Himalayas
By Phuntsok Namgyal, ISBN: 1-931907-02-1, Hardcover,
Art/Architecture, $39.95

A magnificent and spectacular photographic book about the Potala Palace, the palace of the Dalai Lamas and the world's highest and largest castle palace. Over 150 rare and extraordinary color photographs of the Potala Palace are showcased in the book, including murals, thang-ka paintings, stupa-tombs of the Dalai Lamas, Buddhist statues and scriptures, porcelain vessels, enamel work, jade ware, brocade, Dalai Lamas' seals, and palace exteriors.

Breaking Grounds: The Journal of a Top Chinese Woman Manager in Retail by Bingxin Hu, Preface by Louis B. Barnes, Harvard Business School, ISBN: 1-931907-15-3, 256pp, Hardcover, Business, $24.95

The book records the experience of a Chinese business woman who pioneered and succeeded in modernizing the aging Chinese retail business. Based on her years of business experience, the author recounts the turmoil, clashes of concepts and behind-the-scene decisions in the Chinese retail business, as well as psychological shocks, emotional perplexes, and intellectual apprehension she had gone through.

www.homabooks.com

ORDERING INFORMATION: U.S.: $5.00 for the first item, $1.50 for each additional item. **Outside U.S.**: $12.00 for the first item, $6.00 for each additional item. All major credit cards accepted. You may also send a check or money order in U.S. fund (payable to Homa & Sekey Books) to: Orders Department, Homa & Sekey Books, P. O. Box 103, Dumont, NJ 07628 U.S.A. Tel: 800-870-HOMA; 201-261-8810. Fax: 201-384-6055; 201-261-8890. Email: info@homabooks.com

Printed in the United States
134679LV00003B/1/P